Praise for *The Zen of Social Media Marketing*

"*The Zen of Social Media Marketing* demystifies the wacky, yet immensely powerful new world of online conversational marketing and serves as a great primer to understand where to allocate your time, money, and energy. A great read for entrepreneurs, professionals, and small business."

—Jonathan Fields, Author of *Career Renegade*

"Building on a strong background of expert marketing advice, Shama has again produced a body of work that is at once complete and practical. This is a book that you can read quickly when you're frustrated by what seems like endless contradictions of social media, and then referenced again and again as you develop your own sense of place on the social web. It is, after all, quite correctly titled *The Zen of Social Media Marketing*. I highly recommend this book."

—Dave Evans, Social Media Strategist,
and Author of *Social Media Marketing: An Hour a Day*

"Shama breaks down the 'why' and 'how' with easy-to-understand examples that can get you on the right track immediately...and ultimately grow your business."

—Joe Pulizzi, Coauthor of *Get Content. Get Customers*,
and Founder of Junta42

"Finally! A true authority on the subject of social media has broken through the utter noise of get-rich-quick-with-social-media hysteria. Shama takes the mystery and hype out of social media and gives readers a practical step-by-step action plan to start, grow, measure, expand, and optimize their online presence. It is a must-read for any marketing professional, C-level executive, or entrepreneur. Her conversational writing style, numerous case studies, and 'how-to' guides with screen shots make learning and implementing almost elementary. It will be *required reading* for all our clients."

—Joe Abraham, Founder and Managing Director at En Corpus Group, and Author of *B.O.S.I. Entrepreneurship*

"Ready for a *true* social marketing awakening? If so, be sure and take Shama Kabani's *The Zen of Social Media Marketing* on your path to web enlightenment."

—Dean Lindsay, Author of *The Progress Challenge* and *Cracking the Networking CODE*

"*The Zen of Social Media Marketing* is a comprehensive guide for maximizing the marketing opportunities from online networks. Shama Kabani helps you make the most of your efforts in marketing through a stronger knowledge of social media."

—Penelope Trunk, Founder of the Social Network Brazen Careerist

---

"Shama is hands-down the industry leader in social media marketing and creating buzz. She has a rare combination of social media savvy and law-of-attraction mastery that businesses clamor to find. It's easy to see why she's called the 'Shaman of social media.' She will transform your marketing and increase your sales. Listen to everything this luminary says."

—Shawne Duperon, Five-Time EMMY® Award Winner, ShawneTV

"*The Zen of Social Media Marketing* is for anyone that has ever felt overwhelmed by all of the online options available now for networking, socializing, and just plain being online in general! Shama breaks it down so that even the most social media–phobes will be breathing sighs of relief at how simple she makes it all sound! Get this book today and be on your way to a stress-free online experience that you will groove and align with, thrive, and enjoy."

—Sally Shields, Author of *The DIL Rules*

The Zen of
Social Media
MARKETING

An Easier Way to Build Credibility,
Generate Buzz, and Increase Revenue

....

Shama Kabani

BENBELLA BOOKS, INC.

DALLAS, TEXAS

BenBella

BenBella Books, Inc.
10300 N. Central Expressway, Suite 400
Dallas, TX 75231
www.benbellabooks.com
Send feedback to feedback@benbellabooks.com

Printed in the United States of America
10 9 8 7 6 5 4 3 2 1

Library of Congress Cataloging-in-Publication data is available for this title.
ISBN 978-1-937856-15-1

Copyediting by Rebecca Logan and Deb Kirkby
Proofreading by Erica Lovett, Gregory Teague, Chris Gage, and Christine Koch
Cover design by Faceout Studio, Tim Green
Text design and composition by John Reinhardt Book Design
Printed by Berryville Graphics, Inc.

Distributed by Perseus Distribution
http://www.perseusdistribution.com/

To place orders through Perseus Distribution:
Tel: (800) 343-4499
Fax: (800) 351-5073
E-mail: orderentry@perseusbooks.com

Significant discounts for bulk sales are available.
Please contact Glenn Yeffeth at glenn@benbellabooks.com or (214) 750-3628.

Contents

Acknowledgments

This book has been a team effort. I couldn't have done it without the following individuals, who guest wrote, edited, and guided me throughout the process:

Rilee Chastain (Google+), Stephanie Cross (Websites and Blogging), Natalie Bidnick (Twitter), Dave Kaminski (Web Video), Katherine Lockhart (Facebook), Albert Maruggi (Social Advertising), Idan Shnall (SEO), Jill Brockmann (Discussion Questions), my agent Janet Goldstein, and my publisher BenBella Books.

This book is just as much theirs as it is mine.

Our clients at the Marketing Zen Group: Thank you for allowing us to guide you online. Thank you for your trust, your respect, and your belief in the Marketing Zen Group.

Arshil Kabani: Thank you, honey, for being the wind beneath my wings.

Foreword

Shama Kabani starts off her book with a scene from *The Matrix*. I know the scene well. It's a little bit of philosophy thrown into Hollywood and made simple to consume. Shama's right for giving us this gem; *The Matrix* seems to have motivated a lot of us to think differently about how we live online, and how business works.

I know. I wrote about *The Matrix* a few different times in *Trust Agents*. We could have just written, "To be a trust agent is to know how to be Neo," and it would've been a shorter book.

There is a Zen to social media. There is a way. Shama's right about that. And her way—her thoughts, her experiments, her recommendations in this book—is one that can get a lot of people closer to the prize than anything they might intuit and do on their own.

Business rules are different now. Don't believe me? How are the banks in the United States doing? How are the three big carmakers? How are small businesses doing? You want to keep marketing the way companies have been for the last fifty years? Not a good idea, I'm afraid.

We're writing new code, and Shama knows it.

There's human code out there all about how human you can be, how you can connect with people, and what that means for business. I'm flying all over the planet right now writing new versions of this code for companies, showing them how to be human. The goal is simple: explain to people that, while face-to-face is just as important as it ever was, now we've got all kinds of new tools that let us tighten bonds in between those in-person moments.

These tools leave a wake of data behind them. Follow these invisible trails of data and you can smell new customers, new opportunities. New networks don't form inside your inbox. New phone numbers don't start following you (frankly, that's probably a good thing). Social media provides the links and connections that allow these networks to form. I've taken to calling Twitter the Serendipity Engine, because that's what it harnesses: serendipity. And you, too, can harness it for your business.

Shama has a way of teaching this new code—her business-savvy Zen approach—that fits the business you're in, the person you are, and the results you want. I might do a few things differently, but we all might. (After all, if you see Buddha on the road, kill him. Isn't that the quote?) And you need to consider what parts of her approach you'll benefit most from implementing. But ignoring her isn't a good move.

Get into *The Zen of Social Media Marketing*. Keep a notepad file handy. Write down notes. Seek out everything that makes sense for you. Start setting up some next moves based on what you learn. Shama will show you.

Meanwhile, I'm waiting for the white rabbit.

—Chris Brogan,
coauthor of the *New York Times*
and *Wall Street Journal* best seller *Trust Agents*

Introduction

Why Write This?

When the first edition of *The Zen of Social Media Marketing* came out in April 2010, I was truly humbled by the amazing response we received. Readers from every walk of life and every corner of the world sent me their stories, their challenges, and their questions. Two years later, I knew the vast world of social media had changed enough to require an updated guide. Although the principles of online marketing and social media remain unchanged, new platforms, opportunities, and tools have emerged that make marketing online more efficient and easier than ever.

Social media is now an integral part of everyday life. Yet many continue to struggle with it.

A while back, I realized the *main* reason people are struggling with social media marketing: they are going against the natural order of things! The traditional marketing rules cannot be applied to social media because social media is not a marketer's platform. It belongs to consumers.

For the longest time, marketing consisted of putting out a message about a business or product that was controlled strictly by the business itself. Think about a square peg. The square peg represents the traditional marketing message. Now, imagine square holes. Each hole is a traditional marketing medium—print, radio, and television. The square peg fits the square hole perfectly.

However, here comes social media: multiple online mediums all controlled by the people participating within them—people who are busy having conversations, sharing resources, and forming their own communities. Social media is full of constant activity controlled by no one individual in particular. Unlike radio, television, and print, it isn't passive—users don't just receive content; they create it, too. Social media is a circular hole. Yet most marketers are still using a square peg. They are working *against* the grain. And they're finding themselves thoroughly stumped and no better off than they were when they started on their journey.

I wanted something I could hand to these frustrated folks, something that could help social media make *sense* to them. I **wanted something that would finally help marketers (and make no mistake—we are all marketers) understand how to utilize social media marketing concepts in a practical and efficient manner. I wanted to help them find the circular peg to fit the circular hole.**

I wanted to show them the *Zen* of social media marketing. Once you truly understand how social media functions, marketing using social media channels becomes effortless.

The Zen of What?

Yes, I know. Spending hours on social media sites only to be disappointed by a zero return on your investment doesn't put you in a Zen-like state. But that happens *only* if you are doing it wrong! If you go with the flow, you can rake in the profits *and* have fun. Imagine that!

The Zen of Social Media Marketing **is about understanding the mind-set of people who are using social media and then using it to your advantage.**

Do you remember the famous scene from *The Matrix* where Neo bends the spoon? It went like this:

> **Spoon boy:** Do not try and bend the spoon. That's impossible.
>   Instead...only try to realize the truth.
> **Neo:** What truth?
> **Spoon boy:** There is no spoon.
> **Neo:** There is no spoon?

Spoon boy: Then you'll see that it is not the spoon that bends; it is only yourself.

Social media is like that spoon. If you try to bend it, it won't bend. If, instead, you bend—if you alter your own attitude and how you market—you win. Have you ever wondered how some people rack up friends and followers, cultivate fans, and just seem to be *everywhere* at once? These people are true Zen marketers. They may not even realize they're doing anything special; they just go with the flow. They make it look effortless because so much of it *is* effortless.

Now, if you are thinking this book is just going to tell you to breathe deeply and use the force, think again. Like every good Zen master, you need some tools in your arsenal. In the following pages, I will share with you all the tools and techniques you need to become the ideal social media marketer—the guy or gal people want to be friends with and whose business gets talked about constantly.

A Personal Story

I launched my online marketing firm, The Marketing Zen Group, right out of graduate school, on my own with no resources. Today, we have a full-time team of thirty and a global clientele. And 100 percent of our clients came to us from our online marketing efforts, specifically our social media marketing efforts. Today, we are recognized as one of the leading digital marketing companies in the world.

I continued to hire the best people to help grow our team until we became a truly full-service web agency. Whatever our clients needed online, we could provide. Soon, the business fueled its own growth. Word spread quickly; that's the nature of online marketing! I started receiving invitations to speak at top industry conferences, earned interviews with television media, and we had to start turning *away* more clients than we were taking on. As the business grew, so did my personal brand. I am humbled by and grateful for our growth.

My company is living proof that, when done right, social media marketing *works* for businesses. And it works, albeit slightly differently, for businesses of all sizes and types. I know this because we have worked with clients at all stages—from start-ups to Fortune 500s—to leverage social media. **It is my sincerest intention to share with you the same wisdom that helped our company and our clients' companies grow.** Throughout this book, you will find the stories of businesses from a variety of industries that are successfully marketing through social platforms. If they can do it, so can you!

Who Is This Guide a Perfect Fit For?

If you are responsible for marketing in any shape or form, this guide is written for you. Perhaps you are a small business owner responsible for attracting your own customers or clientele, or the CEO of an Inc. 5000 company that wants to solidify its online reputation. Or perhaps you're a CMO looking to constantly generate inbound leads. Maybe you want to get the word out about your nonprofit. It doesn't matter; the principles are all the same. This book will show you exactly how to leverage social media to accomplish your goals.

What *does* matter is that you are

- committed to marketing or promoting your service/product/blog/organization in an ethical and unassuming manner;
- willing to listen, communicate, and share (the building blocks of social media marketing); and
- *okay* with doing things the easy way and don't insist on going against the grain.

Social media marketing does *not* have to be a struggle.

Who Is This Guide *Not* a Good Fit For?

This guide is *not* for those who want to become overnight millionaires, internet marketers looking to turn a quick buck, or those looking to grow their Facebook friend count so they can spam those friends. Sorry to disappoint you! The strategies and techniques I lay out in this book are for legitimate businesses that will apply them with consistency and commitment—two necessary elements for social media success.

What Will You Learn?

✓ Where social media marketing fits in the bigger scheme of things
✓ How to make your website or blog the hub of your online marketing efforts
✓ How to use Facebook, Twitter, and LinkedIn for online marketing in an ethical manner
✓ How to drive traffic to your sites
✓ How to use Google+—and Google's other growing tools
✓ How to leverage social advertising—including group-buying websites
✓ How to build credibility and establish expertise
✓ How to generate leads
✓ How to build your own community of fans
✓ How to build your e-zine/newsletter list
✓ How to measure your social media marketing efforts
✓ How to pitch bloggers and engage in Digital PR
✓ How to find and create strategic joint venture relationships using social media
✓ How to leverage your past success to gain future customers and clients
✓ How to get speaking engagements
✓ What you *must* have *before* you start social media marketing
✓ The #1 reason people fail at social media marketing and how to avoid that mistake

Case Studies and Profiles

In addition to the case studies peppered throughout the book, you will find a group of profiles at the end. These profiles present *real* people and businesses using social media marketing to achieve their goals. They aren't all marketers by profession but are marketing and promoting their causes successfully nonetheless.

Here's to you—a future Zen master of social media marketing! Let the journey begin.

Online Marketing Basics

BEFORE WE LOOK AT ONLINE MARKETING, let's look at traditional or offline marketing. This will help set the foundation for marketing on the internet. Before the advent of the internet, there were predominantly three main ways to market. These traditional marketing avenues were print, TV, and radio. Print included newspapers, magazines, Yellow Pages, posters, billboards, and even direct mail. Radio and TV included commercials and spots or segments. Traditional marketing worked very well for many years for three main reasons.

REASON 1: Marketing was a one-way street. Companies talked at the consumers, and this was expected because there really was no viable way for customers to talk back. Sure, word of mouth existed. However, you would realistically only tell Joe, Sally, and maybe Mary (if she was in town) before moving on. Moreover, it took a long time for word to get around. So, basically, if the nice-looking lady on television said the laundry detergent was amazing, we believed it. Today, we can go on a company's Facebook page, find them on Twitter, or even comment on their blog. Customers can—and are—talking back!

REASON 2: We were all the same, more or less. Let's face it! We wore the same clothes, had the same habits, and enjoyed the same activities. It was easier for marketers to target buyers because they knew exactly who and where they were. Targeting a woman in her thirties? She was most likely a married mother of two and a stay-at-home mom. She put her family first and most likely went to church on Sundays. Try targeting a woman in her thirties today. She *may* be a stay-at-home mom to two kids and go to church on Sundays. But she may just as likely be a single woman focused on her career who enjoys hiking on the weekends. Today, you need a multipronged approach. You can't reach a demographic through one channel. You have to reach people through the channel of their choice.

REASON 3: We were less tired—and a little less jaded. At first, we believed the man on television when he said that his product could eliminate any stain. We believed it when the woman who reminded us of Grandma said the cookies tasted freshly baked. We believed it all—for a while. We were so transfixed by the well-written copy in the magazine or the flashy ad on TV. Today, we are a lot savvier. We check reviews, leave comments, and demand trial versions.

Does this mean traditional marketing is over? Not at all. It has, however, evolved. The internet has woven its way through every form of traditional marketing. When was the last time you got a piece of direct mail that didn't have a website address for you to visit? Every morning I listen to NPR (National Public Radio), and every morning the broadcasters invite me to tweet them my questions or fan their Facebook page.

What is online marketing? Online marketing is the art and science (dare I say the Zen?) of leveraging the internet to get your message across so that you can move people to take action. Whether that action is donating their time to your cause or buying your product or service, the goal of marketing has always been the same—to get people to take action. The tools just keep changing.

If online marketing is the act of leveraging the internet in general to get your message across, social media marketing is the act of leveraging specifically social media platforms (places where

The social media movement has provided the business owner powerful tools for reaching thousands of prospects and clients at the click of a mouse. However, without a strong business strategy and knowledge of online marketing, these tools are often used in vain. Success in this new media requires you to lead with a strong business mind-set.

To that end, ask yourself:

- What exactly am I trying to accomplish with social media and why?
- What are my readers' most pressing challenges, and how can I help them overcome these?
- What are the most effective delivery tools for my messages?
- How can I build enduring relationships and turn strangers into lifetime customers?

Mitch Meyerson,
author of Mastering Online Marketing *and eight other books*
(www.MitchMeyerson.com)

people connect and communicate) to promote a product or a service to increase sales.

First I want to share with you a simple framework for marketing online. This framework is necessary because social media marketing is not a stand-alone process or an outcome. So, before we delve into the specifics, we have to take in the big picture.

Successful online marketing can be broken down into three distinct components. I like to use the acronym ACT to describe the process.

The ACT Methodology

CONVERT

Successful
Online
Marketing

ATTRACT

TRANSFORM

A is for Attract. To attract means to get attention or stand out. Practically, this means attracting traffic to your website—your main online marketing tool.

C is for Convert. Conversion happens when you turn a stranger into a consumer or customer. And there is a difference between the two! A consumer may take in your information or even sample your product, but he or she may not always buy. That's okay! Over time, that consumer may become a customer. The more expensive a purchase is, the longer it may take. This means that you constantly have to work to convert people into consumers *and* customers.

T is for Transform. You transform when you turn past and present successes into magnetic forces of attraction.

Let's use Sue as an example. Sue sells quilts on the internet. So do hundreds of other people. How can Sue bring people to her website? If she has a Facebook page, she could create an album of her quilts. Jane, a Facebook friend of Sue's, looks at the pictures and instantly thinks of getting one for her granddaughter. She sees that Sue has placed a link to her website right below the pictures, so she clicks over to her site. Sue has successfully ATTRACTED Jane to her website.

With social media, you are the publisher! The sooner you realize you are a publisher, the more successful your business will be. Wouldn't it be great if people relied on you and your business to help them in their careers and personal lives? It's possible, but you have to start thinking differently about the way you market. Publishing valuable, relevant, and compelling information targeted to your customers and prospects is the answer. What's your expertise? How does that expertise relate to your customers' pain points? Then create the story and reach people where they are—through email, ebooks, blogs, social media, and more. Then watch the magic happen: you become the authority for that niche. You are the expert, and you may never have to actively sell again!

Joe Pulizzi,
coauthor of Get Content. Get Customers

Once Jane visits Sue's website, she takes a closer look at the quilts. She finds one that she thinks her granddaughter would just love as a holiday gift. She makes a note to herself that she will make sure to come back closer to Christmas. Now, what are the chances that Jane will actually be back? Very slim. Luckily, Sue has a newsletter sign-up box on her home page. She offers Jane some tips on quilt making in exchange for her email address. Jane gladly gives it; she is CONVERTED from a stranger to a consumer. Now, Sue can email Jane whenever she has something exciting to share—a new shipment, some more tips, or even news of a sale. Come Christmas, Jane receives an email from Sue reminding her to get her Christmas shopping done—and Jane buys. She is CONVERTED from a consumer into a customer.

Jane loves the quilt she receives from Sue! It even has a nice note. Jane's granddaughter loves the quilt just as much. In fact, she drags it around the house. It has become her favorite blankie. Jane just has to take a picture and send it to Sue. Sue takes this picture and shares it on her company blog. She TRANSFORMS the success with a customer into an attraction tool. She explains how each quilt leads to long-lasting memories and how happy it makes her to see her customers happy. Enter Don. Don has been thinking about purchasing a quilt for his own daughter but wasn't sure if she would really enjoy it. He just stumbled across Sue's blog after his wife forwarded him an article in which Sue was featured. Seeing Jane's granddaughter's smiling image with the quilt makes Don smile. He thinks, "If that little girl loves it so much, perhaps mine will, too." He also notes how much Sue seems to care about her customers. He buys a quilt instantly.

AHA! Zen Moment

In this book I'll be using the words "customer" and "client" interchangeably to refer to both, because there isn't much difference between them when it comes to using social media marketing techniques: you can ATTRACT, CONVERT, and TRANSFORM both with the same methods! 🙏

Through the ACT process, Sue ensures that she will never be short of customers. It is a simple yet effective process.

Start thinking about *all* your online marketing tactics as falling into *at least one* of these categories. Whenever you think about marketing, ask yourself this question: *Am I using this technique to Attract, Convert, or Transform?* Keep in mind that there are plenty of instances in which an online marketing tactic can perform multiple functions. We will cover these instances later.

Attract

Nowhere is social media marketing *more* successful and useful than in the "attracting" phase of online marketing. During the attraction phase, you are trying to drive traffic to your site and stand out from the masses.

We will look at the *how* of driving traffic later in the book. For now, let's focus briefly on what you *need* in order to make your product or service attractive online.

This may seem like a detour from social media marketing, but it is in fact the framework you *absolutely* must have to attract people to your product or service.

What do you need to attract prospects online? A great BOD!

- **Brand:** If your brand could be summed up in one word, what would it be? I will use my company, The Marketing Zen Group, as an example. Our clients use many words to describe us, but at the end of the day, the best phrase is "full service." We constantly aim to provide anything our clients may need relating to digital marketing and PR.
- **Outcome:** What's the outcome you help clients achieve? Not the process you use but the *final* result. Sum it up in one line: *Our company helps businesses grow by leveraging the internet.* Simple. We may create websites and conduct social media trainings and so on, but those are all part of the process. We do those things to accomplish a goal. That goal is to help our clients make more money. That goal is our outcome.
- **Differentiator:** What makes you *inherently* different from your competitors? The online marketing field is a competitive one. However, most marketing companies only offer one piece of the puzzle. They may offer graphic design, or optimize websites, or focus on simply consulting. There isn't anything wrong with this approach, but this is where our company, The Marketing Zen Group, decided to stand out. We recognized that many clients out there didn't have the time or in-house resources to handle their web marketing. Moreover, they didn't want to hire and manage

multiple companies and consultants. So, we offered to literally take over web marketing for our clients. In essence, we offered to become their online marketing department and drive inbound leads. It has been an amazing differentiator for us! So, your differentiator, in other words, is simply what makes you stand out.

I can't stress enough how important these principles—these basic building blocks—are to online marketing and social media marketing in particular. There is no lack of information and noise out there. As consumers, we are constantly inundated with data.

The branding principle "everything communicates" has only been magnified by the rise of social media.

To be effective in this space, you have to be clear about what you want to be known for—what your brand stands for. And then, you have to be vigilant about building an integrated marketing presence that supports your identity consistently. Due in part to the blurring of personal and professional identities online, you can "leak" messages that are incongruent with your brand. Frustrated offenders might say, "I didn't want *that* to communicate!" But it's not our choice; the experience of the target audience determines our identity, and *they* decide what to include as an element of our brand.

From its essence to its look and feel, business model, affiliations, and so on, it has never been more important to thoroughly plan your brand.

Samantha Hartley,
Enlightened Marketing (www.EnlightenedMarketing.com)

It is a continual grand bazaar. If you don't have the right elements, you can't stand out from the noise. If you don't stand out, you can't attract people to do business.

The #1 reason people fail at social media marketing is that they don't have a solid foundation. They don't have a brand, they don't understand the outcome they provide, and they have absolutely no way of differentiating themselves from the competition.

Social media is the ultimate amplifier. If you have a good product or service, it will be amplified until it is perceived as great.

If you have a shoddy product to begin with, that will also be amplified. Think about when you speak to your friends. Do you tell them that a restaurant you liked was *good* or do you say it was *amazing*? Inside each of us is a storyteller. We like to amplify. Social platforms and the internet in general allow us to do that. They are a megaphone for your message. The people who consistently do well using social media are the ones who were already doing well to begin with. The medium simply amplifies their success.

Convert

So, what happens after you attract clients or customers? If they are an ideal fit, they convert. I say *if* they are an ideal fit because not everyone you attract will be. In our story earlier, Sue attracted Jane, who was an ideal fit. She was looking for quilts to buy. Let's say Sue also attracts Edgar to visit her site because he likes the pictures of the quilts on her Facebook profile. However, he doesn't have any use for a quilt; he just thinks they are pretty. He may never buy. And that's okay. You want to convert the Janes out there, not the Edgars.

As I mentioned previously, conversion can happen in one of two ways: (1) a stranger turns into a consumer, or (2) a stranger turns into a client or customer.

People become consumers when they subscribe to your blog, get on your newsletter list, or merely like your Facebook page (more on this later). They are *consuming* your information. At this point, they have converted. They are no longer strangers.

Why is this important? Even if they aren't paying for the content they're consuming, they are still being exposed to your company and your brand. There is an old marketing adage that says a person must come into contact with your brand seven times before he or she will make a purchase. Seven times!

Think about the last time you went grocery shopping at a big chain store. Chances are that there was some table setup that allowed you to sample a product—whether it was a new juice or old-fashioned jam. Studies show that when people sample, they are more likely to buy! This same "sample table" concept also works online. Offering people a sample of your work—whether through written content, pictures, or videos—can also lead them to buy from you.

Ideally, the formula works like this:

$$\textbf{Consumption of Valuable Content + Time = Client}$$

Time is a variable. Some people may buy right after sampling your product or service. Others may need much longer. Some of our clients received our newsletter for over a year before they decided to become clients. And not *everyone* should turn into a client. You only want those who are a perfect fit. The more qualified the buyer, the fewer the returns.

Consumers and business buyers want to make up their own minds about what they need without interference from noisy marketers. In fact, by the time they are ready to talk to you, they will be armed with information about your company, its people, and its products.

Benefit from this new buyer behavior by engaging with them as they search for answers. Deliver content that is relevant and compelling in their search for solutions. You can do this before they ever call you or walk through your front door.

You become the expert your future buyers can count on. Your content engenders a trusted relationship that makes it easy to buy from you. That's what content marketing is all about.

Newt Barrett,
coauthor of Get Content. Get Customers

How Does Social Media Marketing Fit When It Comes to Conversion?

Let's be completely honest about what social media *rarely* does—lead to instant clients. For example, if you are looking to put up your LinkedIn profile and immediately get swamped by client requests, you may be disappointed. I won't say that social media marketing doesn't ever lead directly to clients because it does happen, but this should not be your goal. If you want to gain clients quickly, there are better ways of achieving it.

What social media is great at is turning strangers into *consumers*. It's the perfect channel for allowing people to get a taste of your product or service—it's sampling made easy.

AHA! Zen Moment

Social media marketing works best as a tool for attracting traffic and attention. It doesn't work as well for converting strangers into clients. It's better suited to converting strangers into consumers (i.e., blog readers or newsletter subscribers), if simply because "free" is an easy sell. Free works! And over time, it can and will lead to business. 🧘

What's the Best Conversion Tool?

Your website! There is *no* getting around this one. You shouldn't be engaging in social media marketing if you *don't* have a website first. Every time I speak on the subject of social media marketing, someone inevitably asks me, "Can't I substitute a social media profile (say, on Facebook or LinkedIn) in lieu of a website?" The answer is *always* no.

Why should you have your own website and not depend on social media profiles?

- **You *own* your website.** You don't own your social media profiles. Your profile (and your hard-earned contact list) is owned by the social media site itself. If it goes "poof" tomorrow, then so does your online presence.
- **Social media profiles are limiting.** You can convey only so much information on your profile. Although it may (and should) intrigue someone, it isn't enough to make a sale. Remember, social media is not a selling tool! It is an attracting tool.

Transform

Once you have mastered the art of attracting and converting, you must transform your successes into attraction magnets. This brings the entire online marketing process full circle.

People, especially strangers, crave social proof. Social proof is the theory that we are more likely to do something when we see others doing it. This applies even *more* when the others in question are similar to us. We often decide what to do (including whether to buy) based on what others are doing. This isn't the only factor in our decision making, but it is a major one.

Social media is built on social proof. Because of this, social media is a great way to transform past successes into new attention for your company.

There are two parts to transforming:

1. **You have to do a good job.** If your service or product just doesn't deliver, you are out of luck. You can't transform a bad experience into an attraction tool. Let's say you sell a blender and it breaks. The customer tries to return it, but your overworked employee says you just don't take returns. Sorry. And good day! This is not an experience you want amplified. On the other hand, if you do a great job, it makes for the perfect story. One of our clients is K9Cuisine.com. They sell premium dog food online. Nothing too glamorous, but their customer service is amazing. They go above and beyond just delivering an order. If a client orders regular shipping, they upgrade it for no extra charge. If a customer says his dog didn't like a specific brand, they swap it out and help him find something that his dog will like. They're more than just a dog food seller; they become trusted dog nutrition advisors who care about your four-legged friend.

2. **You have to *use* your success to attract more success.** This goes beyond just regular testimonials. This involves telling your customers' *story*—the story of what they achieved

through your service or product. When K9Cuisine.com receives an email thanking them for helping Jack, the loved golden retriever, start eating again after a long illness, they ask the customer if they can share their story with others. The story then makes its way onto their Facebook page and into their tweets. Soon, lots of people know about how K9Cuisine.com helped Jack. Next time they think about Fido needing dog food, they will think about K9Cuisine. com. If they have a great experience, they may tell their friends. The cycle continues.

Traditional marketers didn't worry about who controlled the message. Online marketers today engage an empowered customer. For this reason I ask my clients to keep two principles in mind at all times:

1. Make it easy to buy. This involves telling the right story, exposing the real benefits, and making your shopping cart a one-click affair. It helps keep you focused when you are creating your online presence and figuring out how you will construct your marketing message.

2. Pick tactics last. This ensures that you won't get distracted by the latest shiny object fad before you have your essentials in place. Once you do, you can focus on picking the right tactics to really hear your customers.

Stephanie Diamond,
author of Web Marketing for Small Businesses

What Does Social Media Marketing Have to Do with This Step?

Everything! Whereas social media may not be ideal for converting strangers into clients, it's an excellent platform for sharing stories. Stories establish your expertise, attract fresh consumers, and even help convert faster.

The following are possible tools for transformation:

- Testimonials from customers and clients
- Case studies that showcase how a customer found a solution

to his or her problem (ideally the solution is your service or product)
- Video interviews with clients
- Audio interviews with customers
- Pictures of smiling clients with your products

AHA! Zen Moment

Social media platforms are a great way to showcase past and present success stories. By letting the customers speak for themselves, you can leverage social proof to attract more prospects. ⚓

Overview of Online Marketing Tactics and How They ACT (Attract, Convert, Transform)

The following table presents several online marketing methods and how well they accomplish each step of the ACT process. (Note: Search engine optimization [SEO] involves increasing the traffic to a website from search engines by causing the website to appear higher in a list of search results. SEO is discussed in more detail in Chapter 2.)

One-Minute Online Marketing Secret

Method	Attract?	Convert? Consumer or Customer	Transform?
Social media marketing	Yes	Yes: consumer, not customer	Yes
Website/blog/podcast	Yes	Yes: consumer and customer	Yes
Email marketing	No	Yes: consumer and customer	Yes
Giveaway on site to build email list	Yes	Yes: consumer	No
Search engine optimization (SEO)	Yes	Yes: consumer and customer	No
Video	Yes	Yes: consumer and customer	Yes

Have you ever heard of putting strategy before tactics? A strategy is an overall plan. It is the big picture: *what* needs to be accomplished and *why*. Tactics, in contrast, address the *when, where,* and *how*. Tactics are the way you implement your strategy.

Strategy should always come before tactics. However, most people doing business online go about this backwards. I call this the "shiny toy syndrome." They see the next cool networking site and join, or someone tells them they have to have a blog, so they start one only to abandon it after a month. I see people constantly chas-

> The net comprises a gazillion splinters, most of which are businesses trying to claim their spot. So social media doesn't amount to a hill of beans unless what you're promoting stands out in that crowded marketplace. Differentiation is key, and that is why *nothing* can get along in the land of social media marketing without a clearly defined, unique, "hooky" offer. This is actually the most important part of branding—not the clever name or snappy tagline, as most think. In fact, when I brand folks, the brand is added last and naturally tumbles out of the "hooky" offer. My intention in branding folks is always to extract what is truly unique, quirky, interesting, and relevant about them and their businesses and then roll that into the offer and consequently the brand. What's hooky about you?
>
> Suzanne Falter-Barns,
> Get Known Now (*www.GetKnownNow.com*)

ing the next cool thing online without really knowing specifically what they want to accomplish. They may think, "I want to make money," but don't go further than that. And most importantly, because they don't know what they want to accomplish, they don't know how to measure the success of their tactics.

Are you trying to attract? Convert? Transform? Once you decide what your goal is, look at the preceding table to find a tactic that will help you achieve it. Then you'll also know how to measure your success. For example, if you *know* that the ad you are going to put on Google is meant to attract, then you will measure the number of visitors to your site to gauge how successful your investment was. You won't waste your time being frustrated that it didn't lead to more direct sales. If you were using a tactic to convert, you would check the number of people who subscribed to your newsletter. (Hint: These subscribers would be considered consumers! Remember: Consumption of Valuable Content + Time = Client.)

Now that you have a solid understanding of how social media fits into the bigger scheme of things, let's take a quick look at how to make the most of your ultimate conversion tool—your website!

Websites and Blogging

YOUR WEBSITE IS A WINDOW into your company. If eyes are the window to a person's soul, a website is the window to a company's soul. Okay, okay, so now you know why I am sticking to writing nonfiction. My point is your website is crucial.

Social media, blogging, search engine optimization, and email marketing are powerful ways of developing online leads for most business. However, it's your company's website where your prospect makes a buying decision and the sale actually takes place. Each webpage needs to provide prospects with a compelling reason to do business with you, including calls to action that gently direct them down the sales funnel, getting them to "buy now" or contact you. While an unprofessional website will derail the best web marketing campaign, a well-designed site is a powerful conversion tool that will continually deliver high-quality leads.

Rich Brooks,
president of flyte new media (www.flyte.biz)

The following are three reasons you *must* have a website.

REASON 1: It's expected! Can you imagine a business that doesn't have a phone number? No telephone? How 1800s! No website? How 1990s!

As social media grows and companies break new ground, even a website may not be enough. What starts out as "all the cool companies are doing it" soon turns into standard practice. I wouldn't be surprised if future consumers get frustrated because they don't find the company they are trying to reach on Twitter. As communication channels increase, so does our level of expectation.

REASON 2: It's efficient. A website can multiply the number of people your business can influence exponentially.

Let's say you sell art supplies at a beautiful store. How many customers can you serve at one time? Two? Three? Maybe you are really good and you can serve four at a time. How many people can visit your website at once? Hundreds, thousands, maybe even hundreds of thousands. They can see your products, make purchases, and share you with friends—*simultaneously.*

Our website contains everything a prospect might want to know about us. It includes case studies, articles, bios of team members, and even videos! And all of that is available 24/7, whenever our potential clients might need it.

REASON 3: It converts! Perhaps the biggest reason to have a website is that it takes care of the "C" in our ACT blueprint. A website can convert visitors that you attract (using social media) into consumers and customers. You can attract all the people you want on Facebook, Twitter, and LinkedIn. But if they don't convert, what's the point?

Why Your Website Can't Just Be Good—
It Has to Be Great!

Your website is the online equivalent of your office—the place people go when they want to do business with you. It's not enough to have just any website. People expect that your website will match their perception of your business.

Let's say you meet a guy at a party, and he is dressed to the nines. He tells you that he helps business owners triple their income. You also hear from someone else that he is a successful business consultant. You chat with him for a few minutes, and you are impressed! This guy looks like the epitome of success. Then, he pulls out a business card (also fancy) and invites you to his office. You think, "My business could always use more help. It couldn't hurt to visit with this guy." So you go to his office.

Except his office is hard to find. You drive around for thirty minutes in circles before you locate the building, and when you finally find it, it's more like a broken-down warehouse. You park your car, double-check the locks, and slowly make your way in. The office is decrepit. It is a congested little room with papers strewn all around, and to top it off, it smells like cat litter.

Will you still do business with the guy? You might. But you may also see a major disconnect in his public persona and his actual business. If your website isn't up to par—easily findable and professional—this is the same disconnect people are likely to feel about you.

Our web is not the web of the 1990s. Remember when people actually "surfed the internet"? It was common and many times it was listed as a hobby. "I like to read, take long walks on the beach, and surf the internet." Surfing is over. It was easy back then because there were fewer websites. Today, there are trillions of websites, and people have a lot less patience for bad ones. Think about it. How long do you look at a website you are unsure about before you hit the back button? According to Canadian researchers, web users form first impressions of webpages in as little as fifty milliseconds (one-twentieth of a second). In the blink of an eye, we decide if we will keep looking or go back. This is why good enough isn't good enough anymore. You have to have a great website.

Website 911–EMS

To be great, your website must do three things simultaneously. It must Educate, Market, and Sell (EMS). Whenever I hear that someone's website isn't doing what it needs to, I always find it lacking in one of these three areas. And EMS is essential when it comes to conversion.

Imagine that all the visitors to your website are dots on a scale from 1 to 10. At 10, a visitor becomes a client or customer—the ultimate goal. Now, imagine a whole bunch of dots scattered on that scale. Some are at 1, some are at 5, and some are at 9.

The ones at 1 are just being introduced to your brand. They just heard about you and have landed on your website for the first time. They need to be educated about how you work before they will buy. (Note: The bigger a sale, the longer the education process may need to be. You don't think too hard before spending $20 on a book, but you may need more time when you're buying a $20,000 car.)

The people at 5 already know you. They may even trust you. They just need to be nurtured for a while longer. They may need more education, or they may need more marketing—or they may just be waiting for the right time. If you are there when the time is right, the 5s are likely to buy. Let's say you sell Halloween costumes. I may not buy until Halloween comes around, unless another event comes along for which I need a costume. But when I do feel the need, it's important that you are already positioned as a solution.

The 9s may be ready to buy but just need the right incentive. Perhaps a final reminder? A last question answered? A discount? Whatever it is, your website needs to provide it to make the sale.

My goal here is to show you that everyone who visits your

website will be at a different point on that imaginary scale. Your website—through Educating, Marketing, and Selling—has to move all the visitors who are an ideal fit to 10.

Let's take a look at which elements allow a website to serve as the ultimate marketing tool.

Seven Elements of a Great Website

A great website has impeccable design, structure, content, optimization, and maintenance. It also ideally includes a lead capture mechanism and social media integration.

DESIGN: Looks matter—so much so that scientists have a term for the way looks affect us: the halo effect. The halo effect occurs when we think something looks good on the surface and so we broaden the scope of that positive judgment to include characteristics other than outward appearance. If someone is good-looking, we infer that he or she must also have a good disposition. The same concept applies to websites. If a website looks good, we assume that the company behind it must also do good work. First impressions count. Especially online, where a visitor doesn't have much to go by except your website.

LEAD CAPTURE MECHANISM WITH FREE GIVEAWAY: The area on your website where visitors can input their name and email address is called a "lead capture mechanism." The majority of visitors to your website will not purchase right away. It's your job to make sure you give them options that allow you to stay in touch with them. Email marketing is a great way to stay in touch with website visitors and prospects. But when was the last time you were eager to give out your email address? Chances are, your visitors won't be either—unless you provide them with an incentive. A whitepaper, a recorded webinar, or a free report of some type is usually a good choice.

STRUCTURE: Ever visited a website and found yourself struggling to find a page...or even to get back to the home page?

Too many choices boggle the mind. And when our mind is boggled, it is easier to say no than yes. The way you structure your website navigation is crucial. The structure must guide visitors through your website and handhold them (virtually) into taking action. And it must do this for visitors at every level—those who may be ready to buy now and those who are first-time visitors.

CONTENT: Content is king. It is the heart of every good website and serves multiple purposes. The first purpose is to educate prospects and build expertise. This is why blogs are so heralded. A well-written blog can help you stand out from the competition and educate your prospects. (I talk more about blogs later in the chapter.)

You can provide content in several forms: written (blogs and articles), audio (podcasts), and visual (video). Want to really kick it up a notch? Provide content in all three forms. This is not overkill; it's about appealing to the various learning preferences of a potential visitor. In this day and age, choices rule. Give your visitors a choice, and they are much more likely to choose you.

Good content builds trust and credibility with your network. It shows you are keeping up with the latest and greatest trends and information in your industry. It shows you care by sharing resources and tips with your visitors, and it helps you be seen as an expert in your field—the go-to person for all things. The more information you can share, the better. Again, this content should be syndicated throughout your social networks, helping make you a trusted resource.

Content becomes especially important if you are in the professional services industry or any business-to-business field in which expertise plays a key role. Content is also the lifeblood of search engines. Think about it: search engines are looking to serve their customers with good search results. They constantly have to separate the wheat from the chaff. They have to differentiate spam sites (websites set up specifically for the purpose of spamming people—think Viagra emails) from real, wholesome websites (like yours!). One of the ways they do this is by looking for content. The more fresh content you provide to search engines like Google to deliver to their customers, the more the search engines reward you.

SOCIAL MEDIA INTEGRATION: Be sure to make it easy for your visitors to connect with you on the social media networks through your website. Why? Remember, turning strangers into consumers is part of the conversion process. People like to consume information in different formats. One person may prefer to keep in touch with your company on Facebook, although someone else may prefer Twitter, and yet others prefer email marketing. That's why it's important to give website visitors multiple ways to stay in touch.

You also want to make it easy for visitors to share the information with their networks. Having a Facebook "Like" button and a Google+ button on each page of your site for visitors to share information on your website quickly with others is a great way to spread your information as well.

OPTIMIZATION: Optimization has two meanings here. One, your website has to be optimized internally. A website may look beautiful from the outside, but if the inside is poorly built, chances are it will start to show. For example, if it isn't coded correctly, it can look odd in certain browsers even though it looks fine in others. The World Wide Web Consortium has a tool that allows you to make sure your website is well coded. The tool can be found at jigsaw.w3.org/css-validator. You just put in your website address, and it will tell you what, if anything, needs repaired. The second type of optimization relates to search engines and making sure that search engines can "read" your website. This is called search engine optimization, and it is discussed in detail later in the book.

MAINTENANCE: The website of today in many ways is a living, breathing thing. In the past, you could create a website and sit back. Today, you can't. Passively keeping a website is almost akin to opening a store, stocking the shelves, and then doing nothing. You don't have to re-create the store every day or even every year, but you do need to tag products, move items around, change displays, and so on. Your website is the same way. Once you have the design and structure in place, you don't have to keep changing it. However, you do need to maintain it by adding content.

AHA! Zen Moment

Blogging can be a great attracting *and* converting tool! People can find your posts attractive and subscribe to your blog, becoming instant consumers. Over time, they can be converted into customers. 🧘

A blog is an instantly and easily updatable website. A blog is the hub of your social media strategy, enabling you to grow your online presence as social media trends change and evolve.

Andy Wibbels,
author of BlogWild! A Guide for Small Business Blogging

Blogging

All blogs are websites—they exist on the web, and are reached using a web address—but not all websites are blogs. Blogs have these elements in common:

- Content is regularly updated. Search engines love this!
- Content is generally broken down into "posts" (akin to articles).
- Posts are presented in a reverse chronological order (newest first).

- Readers can leave comments. This is excellent for interacting and building a fan base.
- Content is syndicated (published in multiple places at the same time) via an RSS (Really Simple Syndication) feed, allowing people to subscribe to your blog. Every blog has its own unique RSS feed. Anyone can subscribe to your blog's RSS feed and read it using a "feed reader" or a "feed aggregator." There are lots of different feed readers out there. My favorite is Google Reader, which can be found at www. google.com/reader.

─────── AHA! Zen Moment ───────

RSS feeds can allow you to distribute the same content to more than one location. You can have wide visibility and gain exposure by distributing the same content strategically to multiple social networks. 🧘

The Million-Dollar Question: Do I Need a Blog?

You don't need a blog, but you do need fresh content on an ongoing basis. The best place to put this content is in a blog. Can you choose just to post this information on a webpage? Yes, but it isn't nearly as efficient because readers can't subscribe, and you can't keep up with your consumers to turn them into clients.

Blogsites

You can add a blog to an existing website, but you can also build a website around a blog. I am a huge fan of hybrid websites, or blogsites, where the entire website is built on a blogging platform. There are many blog publishing platforms out there, but the one we use most often is WordPress. It is the most robust platform, and many business websites are now using it as a content management system (CMS). A CMS allows you to manage your entire website like you would a blog. You get an admin

I started my blog four years ago and always had it separate from my business website. Right before my book launched this year, I decided to move to an integrated "blogsite" platform on WordPress for the following reasons:

- **Effort and resources:** It was taking too much time to update both a blog and website with relevant information. And without changing information on the website, why would people come back after an initial visit? By having an integrated site, people come back over and over to read new content.
- **SEO:** I realized that I was not being efficient by driving people to two sites. It became confusing to know which link to provide when sharing my bio, and I was diluting the SEO for both sites. Now every road leads to one site, which has increased traffic and Google ranking.
- **Client conversion:** I had many people visit my blog who loved my posts but who did not have a complete picture of what I did professionally. Many did not click the link in my "About" section to my main website to find out about my products and services. Since converting to one site, I have had a twofold increase in individual coaching clients, as well as strong sales in my live workshops and membership site.

Pamela Slim,
author of Escape from Cubicle Nation

console from which you can edit your site, allowing you to maintain your website and make regular changes without much technical knowledge. If you don't have a technical background or a webmaster who can make your updates, you should consider getting a content management system.

Now, let's say you have an excellent website in place with lots of wonderful fresh content. How do you drive traffic to it? Keep reading...

WordPress is the ultimate publishing platform because it's easy to use, it's not overly complicated, and it's infinitely flexible. Sure, it's great for blogs, and that is its forte, but it's also great for non-blog websites and even ecommerce sites. Because of plug-ins and themes (especially Headway, which includes visual blog design tools), WordPress can be extended into anything you can imagine. Creating and publishing content in WordPress really is about as easy as writing an email, only instead of clicking "Send," you click "Publish." That's such a satisfying button to click on, too, because whenever you do it, you know that hundreds or even thousands of people are going to read what you wrote.

Michael Martine,
Remarkablogger (remarkablogger.com)

Tips for an "Optimal" Blog

There is a strategy to blogging. Here are a few guidelines to follow when blogging to get the biggest bang for your buck:

- Ideally, you should blog two times per week, especially when starting out.
- Each blog post should be a minimum of 500 words.
- Be sure to use keywords in your blog. For example, if you're a manufacturer of baked goods, you want to write posts that are relevant to baking—how to bake a cake, best desserts, and so forth. (You will learn more about keywords in the following chapter covering SEO.)
- Interlink when appropriate. When you have a keyword or phrase in your blog, link it back to the page on your site that talks about that particular product or service. For instance, if you are blogging about tips for ordering a wedding cake, link the words "wedding cake" with the page on your site that talks about wedding cakes. This is a great tip for aiding in your organic search rankings.
- Use a picture in every blog post. You'll be syndicating your blog posts into your different social networks, and when

the blog posts feed into Facebook, as an example, the picture will show up. People are much more likely to read a blog post with a captivating picture than one without a picture. Don't have a relevant image of your own? You can get royalty-free images on flickr.com (just be sure to check the box for Creative Commons/for professional use on the Advanced Search page).

- If using WordPress, be sure to add tags—keywords or phrases for subjects you discussed in your blog. Again, this is a great search engine optimization tool.

Solid content is really at the heart of any good online marketing campaign, and these guidelines can help you optimize your blog content to the fullest!

Search Engine Optimization (SEO)

The Art and Science of Driving Traffic to Your Website

SEARCH ENGINE OPTIMIZATION, also known as SEO, is the process of improving the position and visibility of a website on search engines such as Google, Yahoo!, and Bing. The most important reason to get higher rankings is that you will get more targeted leads and conversions, which in turn means you will get more people knocking on your door to buy your products.

The most beautiful thing about search engine marketing is how targeted it is. Traditional marketing is like a funnel, with a wide top and a small bottom. The top is the whole audience that sees your marketing effort (say, a commercial on TV or radio, or an ad in a magazine or newspaper), and the bottom is the people who might actually be interested in your product or service—the

29

people you actually want to reach. Search engine marketing targets the bottom of the funnel. You don't get a large general audience. You get the audience who is searching for exactly what you're selling. Google will never show a user something that is not relevant to his or her search query. Google and other major search engines will never list your website high on their results page otherwise. The key to getting high search engine ranking for the audience you want is *relevancy*. Your site must appear relevant to a specific search query.

Google, as well as other search engines, uses more than 200 factors in their search engine algorithm to rank webpages. In order for your site to appear at the top of the search engines for specific search queries, you must follow strategic step-by-step guidelines to ensure that your site is search engine friendly and fully optimized for search engines. In this chapter, you will learn how to optimize the pages on your site to get search engines to rank your site as **the most relevant** in the search query or queries your target audience is using, which will lead more business to your website.

You might have heard the saying around SEO blogs and discussion boards that "Content is King," which is true. But optimizing that content is how to ensure your site performs better than your competitors'.

Let's begin our search engine optimization process and discover how you can dominate the Search Engine Results Page with the most competitive keywords for your company.

Keyword Research

One of the most vital steps to take in starting your search engine optimization process is to identify your target audience, and the keywords those potential customers and visitors use in search engines. If you know what your customers are searching for, you will be able to build your site and marketing campaign specifically around those customers and their inquiries.

There are many legitimate keyword tools out there, but for this example we'll use the Google Suggestion Tool, which provides you with keywords users are searching for on Google.com, to identify our target audience and build our keyword research from the ground up.

To launch this tool, go to https://adwords.google.com/select/KeywordToolExternal. The new and improved Google Suggestion tool looks like this:

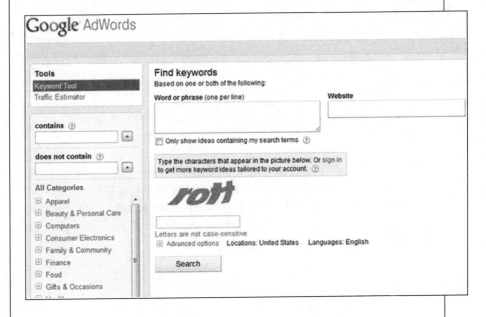

Let's say we're building a site for a company that specializes in fundraising. Type "Fundraising" into the "Find keywords" box and enter the captcha letters (the letters that help a site validate that you are a human and not a virus). Then click on "Search."

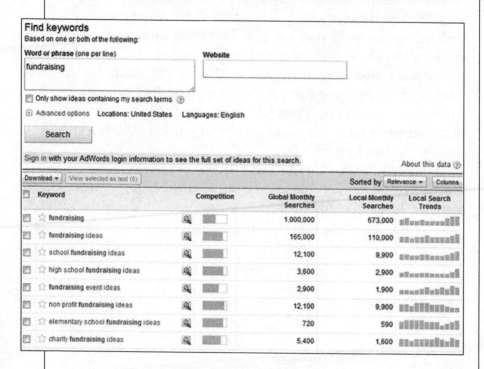

Begin your keyword research by searching for broad keywords. As you continue, drill down to more specific keywords within your industry. This will help you reach a more specific target audience. For example, type in "raise money for" and you will get the following results:

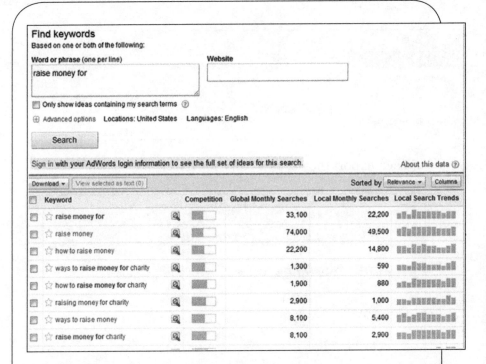

Find keywords
Based on one or both of the following:

Word or phrase (one per line)

raise money for

Website

☐ Only show ideas containing my search terms ⑦
⊕ Advanced options   Locations: United States   Languages: English

[Search]

Sign in with your AdWords login information to see the full set of ideas for this search.   About this data ⑦

Download ▾ | View selected as text (0) | Sorted by Relevance ▾ | Columns |

☐	Keyword		Competition	Global Monthly Searches	Local Monthly Searches	Local Search Trends
☐ ☆	raise money for	🔍	▪▪	33,100	22,200	
☐ ☆	raise money	🔍	▪▪	74,000	49,500	
☐ ☆	how to raise money	🔍	▪▪	22,200	14,800	
☐ ☆	ways to raise money for charity	🔍	▪▪	1,300	590	
☐ ☆	how to raise money for charity	🔍	▪▪	1,900	880	
☐ ☆	raising money for charity	🔍	▪▪	2,900	1,000	
☐ ☆	ways to raise money	🔍	▪▪	8,100	5,400	
☐ ☆	raise money for charity	🔍	▪▪	8,100	2,900	

Notice that there are quite a few searches for keywords such as "how to raise money," "ways to raise money for charity," and "how to raise money for charity." These are all great keywords that you can use to expand your site's content and pages.

Google allows you to download each list of keywords you generate with your searches to a separate file. This is a great process to help you stay organized. When you finish a keyword search session, click on "Download" and then "Download all."

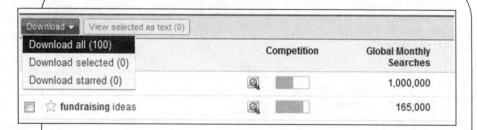

Then export the list as a "CSV for Excel" file.

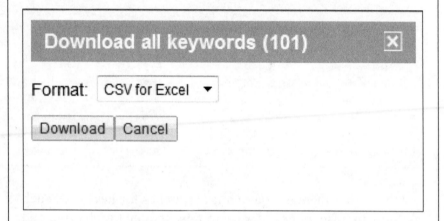

Organize your Excel file by grouping your keywords into categories. Every category will contain a set of keywords associated with it. For example:

	A	B	C
1	Category	Keyword	Global Monthly Searches
2	Fundraising	fundraising	1000000
3	Fundraising	fundraising ideas	165000
4	Fundraising	school fundraising ideas	12100
5	Fundraiser	fundraiser	450000
6	Fundraiser	fundraiser ideas	201000
7	Fundraiser	school fundraiser ideas	14800

The Fundraising category will have keywords such as fundraising, fundraising ideas, and school fundraising ideas. The Fundraiser category will contain the keywords associated with it: fundraiser, fundraiser ideas, school fundraiser ideas, and similar phrases.

Note: You should export all the CSVs and then combine them into one document yourself. This will ensure that you have all your keywords in one spot.

This keyword identification process will assist you throughout the duration of your search engine marketing campaign, as you create new content or edit your existing content to include these keywords.

More Keyword Research

Keyword research is an ongoing process. You can always find and identify other keywords potential customers are searching for as your business grows and develops. In particular, there are two easy-to-use tools that can help you keep your keyword list up to date.

Google's keyword suggestion tool is a great way to identify additional keywords you may have missed. In the following example, we are trying to find additional keywords Google suggests to its users (which are based on what others are currently searching for) when typing "how to raise money":

| how to raise money for charity |
| how to raise money **for charity** |
| how to raise money **fast** |
| how to raise money **for a cause** |
| how to raise money **fast for kids** |

Google suggests that the phrases "how to raise money fast" and "how to raise money online" would be very useful keywords to use in optimizing specific pages on your site tailored to different audiences.

Google's "Searches related to" feature is another tool to identify additional keywords. Go to Google.com and type in "Fundraising ideas." Scroll down the page to the very bottom, and you will see:

Searches related to **fundraising ideas**

unique fundraising ideas	fundraising **events**
non-profit fundraising ideas	**charity** fundraising ideas
sports fundraising ideas	**school** fundraising ideas
high school fundraising ideas	fundraising ideas **college**

These keywords are more useful additions to your list and can help you with further keyword research using Google's keyword suggestion tool. Hang on to this keyword list, because it provides you with greater insight into the minds of your consumers. You can also use your keywords for topic ideas when working on blog posts or content for your website.

Technical Issues with Your Site

Site architecture is your approach to the design and planning of your site. Google, as well as other major search engines like Yahoo! and Bing, pay close attention to how your site is built in order to determine if the site is "good enough" to be listed at the top of the search engine's pages. Everything from your site's navigation menu to hidden files and broken links and more can affect your site's rankings. If your website is not coded correctly, your site's architecture can actually get your website ranked behind your competitors'. It's very important to check certain elements in order to ensure your site is search engine–friendly and ready to be easily "crawled" (reviewed for results page inclusion) by the search engines.

- **Google Webmaster Central:** This tool ensures that your site is search engine–friendly. It will identify various issues, such as broken links, malware, crawling issues, and other problems, as well as providing data on search engine indexing and search traffic. If you sign up for this tool, Google will also send you messages if it finds issues with your current site. To create an account, visit www.google.com/webmasters.

- **Sitemap.xml:** A sitemap is a file that lists all the pages that you want the search engines to crawl; it's like a glossary for Google. Generate a sitemap.xml and upload it to the root directory of your server. Then submit it to Google Webmaster Central.
- **Site speed:** Ensure that your site loads quickly. There are many free tools that can be found online to test loading time. Use them to compare your site to the top sites on the first page of Google. If your site loads slower than your competitors, ask your website developer or programmer to take steps to improve your speed: clean the code your site was written in, reference java script codes, and reduce the size of large images, just to name a few examples. You can also have your programmer check various advanced server issues. However, sharing a server with other websites or webhosts can sometimes cause problems that you might not necessarily be aware of but which slow down your site.
- **Google Analytics:** This tool tracks how visitors are getting to your site and generates advanced traffic reports. To create an account, visit www.google.com/analytics.
- **404 page error:** A 404 page is a custom error page that appears whenever a visitor accidentally arrives on a page of your site that no longer exists or, in some cases, never existed. For example, let's say a visitor was trying to get to your services page, and misspelled the exact URL. A 404 page should come up to help them. This makes for a better user experience, which search engines value. Also, search engines like knowing which pages exist and which don't. Your 404 page should be customized to contain a message to the user telling him or her that the page was not found, plus a call to action to

continue browsing your site, such as alternative pages to visit.

- **301 Redirect**: Google treats http://Domain-Name.com and http://www.Domain-Name.com as two different sites. This means your website's SEO is penalized. To avoid this, create a 301 redirect from Domain-Name.com to www.Domain-Name.com. If you currently have an .htaccess file on the root, simply add the following code to it:

```
RewriteEngine On
RewriteCond %{HTTP_HOST} ^Domain-Name.com [NC]
RewriteRule ^(.*)$ http://www.Domain-Name.com/$1 [L,R=301]
```

(Just make sure your website does in fact redirect to the www. Domain-Name.com after updating the .htaccess page.)

- **301 Permanent Redirect**: If you are redeveloping a website, your pages may end up with new URLs. A 301 permanent redirect ensures the search engines know that your old pages have moved to a new location. If you don't do this, your site may lose the SEO value that your old pages acquired over the years.
- **Robots.txt**: Your site may include data you do not want to be searchable. To ensure that search engines do not crawl and index sensitive information, use a robots.txt file, which tells search engines not to crawl specific areas of your website. You can add the robots.txt file to the Google Webmaster tool.
- **Broken Links**: Search engines don't like when sites link to pages that have been deleted or moved. Ensure that there are no links like this on your site by checking Google Webmaster Central.
- **URL naming**: Use your keywords to create pages dedicated to their target audience. Taking our example for the Fundraising site, you will need to name and create pages using these keywords. For example, if we have a page about

fundraising ideas for schools, name your page schools-fundraising-ideas.html. Remember that search engines are looking for keywords, content, and relevancy to any given unique search query.

- **Image naming:** Naming images is basically the same as URL naming. You want to name your images using the same technique. For example, if you have a page about fundraising for schools, create an image with a fun illustration of kids in school and name your file fundraiser-ideas-for-school.jpg.

On-Page Factors

On-page SEO factors are a crucial part to your site's overall SEO success; they are an integral part of the algorithm Google and other search engines use to rank your page. On-page elements refer to the HTML tags within a site's coding—HTML is a coding language used to write webpages—and they can be tweaked to make your website more appealing to search engines,

Though things like sitemaps and redirects are important, it's best to concentrate on some of the major on-page factors in order to ensure that your webpages are ranked higher with search engines.

Title: The <title> tag defines the title of the page or document online—the way search engines reference your page on their search engine result pages. It's also a great opportunity to provide search engines with information about the page you are trying to optimize.

For example, go to Google.com and type in the following keywords: *fundraising ideas for schools*. You will see the following results:

Ads - Why these a(

New Spring **Fundraiser** - Something Different
www.charlestonwrap.com
Better Quality & Profits
Fundraising Campaign Choices - Shop Now - Request A Free Fundraising Info Kit

Fundraising for **Schools** - Raise Money Online Fast & Easy.
www.fundly.com/**School**-**Fundraising**
$225 Million Raised. High Profits.

BEST **FundRaising** - The Amazing First Aid **FundRaising**™ ✓ Norton
fun**fundraiser**.first-aid-product.com
100%-150% Profit - Fast, Fun, Safe.

Fundraising Ideas - **School** Fundraisers - Fund Raising Events
www.**fundraiser**help.com/
Fundraising ideas for school fundraisers and nonprofit fundraiser events - Find
church fundraiser ideas, youth sports candy sales products, fundraising letters ...
Letters - Top Five Fundraisers - School - Easy Fundraisers

School Fundraisers - **Fundraising Ideas**   ◄——————— Title of Page
www.**fundraiser**help.com/**school**-**fundraisers**.htm
How to information on dozens of **school fundraisers** that produce excellent results -
Articles on elementary **school fundraising**, middle **school** cheerleading ...

School **Fundraising** Ideas for **School** Fundraisers
www.**fundraiser**help.com/**school**-**fundraising-ideas**.htm
Three great **school fundraising ideas** based on simple fundraiser products that
produce excellent fund raising profits.

Here's the HTML code that generated that first title:

<title>Fundraising Ideas – School Fundraisers – High Profit Fundraising</title>

As you can see, the title contains its site's most relevant and important keywords: *Fundraising Ideas* and *School Fundraisers*. These sites are optimized for the search phrase "Fundraising ideas for schools" because of the keywords' proximity in their titles: Fundraising Ideas—School.

Each page of your site should have a unique title that uses three to five keyword phrases and is less than sixty-five characters long. Any characters following the sixty-fifth one will be ignored. You should avoid "stop words" between important keywords such as *and, or, with, for*. You have limited space to write a title and you want to use as many of your main keywords as possible. Dashes are one good way to separate keywords, but do not overuse them. This can be viewed as keyword stuffing (a big no-no) by the search engines. You can use commas, pipe bars, and sentences that make sense to humans, too.

Meta description: The description tag describes, in a couple of sentences, what a page is about. For example:

Snippet of the content from the META description

Fundraising Ideas - **School** Fundraisers - High Profit Fundraising
Easy **Fundraising Ideas** offers the Highest Profit Fundraisers. Unique **fundraising ideas &** products - Fundraising profits as high as 90%!
www.easy-**fundraising-ideas**.com/ - Cached - Similar

Fundraising Ideas - **School** Fundraisers - Fund Raising Events
Fundraising ideas for school fundraisers and nonprofit fundraiser events - Find church fund raisers, youth sports candy sales products, fundraising letters ...
Top Five - School - Letters - Fundraising Event Ideas
www.**fundraiser**help.com/ - Cached - Similar

The HTML code that generated that first link:

<meta name="description" content="Easy Fundraising Ideas offers the Highest Profit Fundraisers. Unique fundraising ideas & products – Fundraising profits as high as 90%! Specializing in school fundraising ideas, sports fundraising ideas and fundraisers for churches and nonprofits." />

When writing a meta description, ensure it is no more than 160 characters in length. Write a unique meta description for each page and the main keywords you are optimizing your page for.

Headings: Search engines use heading tags to tell them of the relative importance of text on a webpage. Your webpage readings should include the most relevant keyword phrases and be wrapped in heading tags, like this:

```
<h1>Most relevant keywords</h1>
<h2>Second most relevant keyword phrases</h2>
<h3>Third most relevant keyword phrases</h3>
```

The best way to optimize the headings on your page is by assigning a heading tag for various relevant paragraphs within your content. The most important tag is the <h1> and is used at the top of the page.

```
<h1>Fundraising Ideas for Schools</h1>
```

The rest of the heading tags can be used for specific short phrases describing the previous tag and the content associated. For example:

```
<h2>Easy Fundraising Ideas for Students in Schools</h2>
```

Follow up with a <h3> heading further down the page that drills down further, such as:

```
<h3>How Do I Start My Own Fundraiser in School?</h3>
```

Keep in mind that your headings must always describe the paragraph or paragraphs that follow it.

Bold, italic, underline, bullet points: Search engines also pay attention to the tags for bold <b>, italic <i>, underline <u>, and bullet points. Use these features to highlight search terms, but be sure to do so tastefully.

Internal linking: One of the best-kept secrets to advanced optimization is internal linking between pages. Internal linking between pages helps Google as well as other search engines understand the relevancy of keywords or keyword phrases to your page content by using what's called "anchor text"—the text that visitors click on to go to another page. For example, let's say you have a page that talks about *fundraising for elementary schools*. This text can be linked to another relevant page on your website that describes *fundraising ideas for kids in school* like this:

```
<a href="http://www.your-domain-name.com/kids-fund-raising-ideas/">Kids Fundraising Ideas</a>
```

Link to page

Anchor text

This is a great way to connect relevant content within a website and target additional keyword phrases.

You may want to use descriptive phrases to link between pages. For example: *the easiest way to raise money for school* would be a great anchor text link to a page that talks about raising money for schools.

Internal linking is also a great way to introduce pages deep within your site (that is, pages that would otherwise take four or more clicks to reach from the home page), so that search engine can crawl and index them.

Image ALT tag: Sometimes, search engines are specifically looking for images, so optimizing your images for these searches can help you reach new customers via image channels like Google Images and Bing Images. The best way to optimize an image is by describing the picture in a few words (focusing on your main keywords, of course). For example, let's say we have an image showing Boy Scouts collecting money for their fundraiser. This would be a good picture to optimize for "boy scouts fundraising ideas." The HTML code will look like this:

```
<img src="boy-scouts-fundraiser.jpg" alt="boy scouts fundraising ideas" />
```

On-page factors are a great way to tell the search engines what your site is about but stay true to your target audience; optimize your pages with the most relevant keywords related to the content of the page. Do not optimize your page for apples when you're talking about oranges.

Link Building

Link building—the process of getting links back to your site placed on other sites in order to increase your site's rank with search engines—is one of the most misunderstood areas of Search Engine Optimization. Let's start by defining what "backlinks" are.

Backlinks are links that point to a website. Let's say a webpage includes the text "RecipesABC has the best chocolate cake recipes in the world" and the words "chocolate cake recipes" link back to www.RecipesABC.com (not an actual site).

What does that mean to search engines?

By providing a link back to RecipesABC.com with the anchor text "chocolate cake recipes," we are telling search engines that RecipesABC.com is relevant to "chocolate cake recipes." The search engines register this as a vote for RecipesABC.com's web popularity, which affects its rank among other relevant sites with the same anchor text "chocolate cake recipes." The more votes to your site, the better rankings your website will achieve when users search "chocolate cake recipes."

Here are a few important factors to remember about link building:

Relevancy: Always seek backlinks from relevant websites. If you have a website that sells a dessert recipe book, make sure to seek links from websites that are relevant to your topic, i.e., other recipe websites, book stores, chef's blogs, home cooking, bakeries nearby, and so on. Their "votes" will mean more to search engines on the subjects you're targeting.

You can use www.dmoz.org to find more topics relevant to the theme of your site.

Website authority: One of the most important things to remember about link building is that not all links are created equal. In the eyes of search engines, a link pointing to your website from the *New York Times* is a lot more authoritative than a link from a website that was created yesterday.

You can use http://who.is to discover who owns a website and when it was created, among other relevant details.

Note: Beware of link farms! A link farm is a website set up with the sole purpose of increasing incoming links for other websites. These sites are usually made up of long lists of unrelated links and are considered a form of spam.

User experience: Google, as well as other search engines, are looking for websites that provide the best user experience. If users can't find what they are looking for, search engines will consider the site less trustworthy. If you see a site that is not so user-friendly, skip your link building efforts there and focus instead on sites that provide a friendlier user experience.

There are many ways to build links back to your site. Here are a few ideas:

- Reach out to relevant blog owners and pitch an interesting story.
- Share your website content on Twitter, Facebook, and Google+, and via quality social bookmarking sites like digg, reddit, and stumbleupon.
- Add sharing options on your website to make it easier for other people to share your stories via social bookmarking sites, social media sites, and email.
- Participate in group discussions and forums related to your industry.
- Participate in Q&A sites, like Yahoo Answers, WikiAnswers, and Quora.

- Contribute to relevant blogs by posting comments on their stories.
- Connect with others whose sites share the same theme or niche as your website and offer them a reason to link back to you.
- Run a promotion or contest on your website. Design a badge and provide the HTML code so your visitors can link back to your website simply by copying and pasting a badge.
- Submit your website to relevant quality directories. Some helpful search terms to consider when looking for relevant directories include:

  {keywords} + "add url"
  {keywords} + "submit url"
  {keywords} + "directory"

- Write press releases about your company and submit them to PRWeb.com and other PR sites.
- Write unique articles related to your industry and distribute them to ezine articles sites, as well as to social media platforms such as squidoo.com and blogger.com.
- Submit your business information to relevant sites like Google Places, Bing Business Portal, Facebook Places, Yelp, Insider Pages, Yellow Pages, and others.

Remember, when asking others to link to you, always request that the link use specific anchor text keywords. This will get your website higher on the search engine results pages for the specific keywords you've been targeting.

Also, always stay relevant by posting only insightful articles and comments on other websites, not spam.

SEO, simplified, consists of this: (1) a well-built website, (2) lots of relevant and timely content, and (3) links back from other credible websites. Don't let the technical aspects overwhelm you too much. Of all web marketing activies, SEO is the most outsourced of them all; the goal for this chapter was just to give you an educated overview. Now, let's move on to social media!

> "Social media marketing is the process of promoting your site or business through social media channels, and it is a powerful strategy that will get you links, attention, and massive amounts of traffic."
>
> Maki,
> *Dosh Dosh*

Social Media Marketing
What You Need to Know Before You Start

The Nature of the Fun-Loving Beast

Now that you have a solid understanding of online marketing, we can move on to social media marketing. Let's break down the phrase "social media marketing."

- **Marketing:** Promoting a product or a service to increase sales
- **Social media:** Online platforms where people connect and communicate

Some examples of online platforms are blogs; social networking sites such as Facebook, Twitter, LinkedIn, and Google+; and YouTube.

Most people abuse social media platforms. They use them to push their message on people and try to dominate the market. Remember our discussion about the mistake of going against the grain? This is a great example. Marketers who abuse social media usually do so because they are used to using traditional marketing methods like television. You can't talk back to the TV. (Well, you can, but it doesn't get you very far.) With social media, talking back is the whole point; it's a conversation, not a monologue.

Chapter 1 discusses how traditional marketing has evolved over the years. Now let's take a look at a table of descriptive words and phrases that compares traditional marketing and online marketing—specifically, social media marketing.

Traditional Marketing	Online Marketing/Social Media Marketing
Dominate the market	Create a community within the market
Shout out loud	Listen, and then whisper
Me, me, me	Us, us, us
Push the product or service	Pull in people with your message/story
Advertising	Word of mouth
Control	Allow
Pursue "leads"	Nurture relationships

Why Social Media Marketing? Why Bother?

According to multiple surveys and studies, between 49 and 90 percent of web users have made a purchase based on recommendations they received through a social media site—an impressive percentage even at the low end. Yet roughly only 25 percent of businesses have a Facebook page, and many fewer use any other social media platforms. Marketers are missing out on a huge opportunity to connect with potential customers. Social media marketing is a good idea for the following three reasons.

1. **Social media sites are where the *people* are.** Let's say there was an expo happening with *750 million attendees*, and I offered you a free booth. Would you take it? I sure hope you would. That's how many people are using Facebook. If Facebook were a country, it would be the world's fourth largest, smaller than the United States but larger than Indonesia. And it costs nothing to join.

2. **Trust in advertising continues to erode.** Let's face it. We trust our friends more than we trust what the nice folks on TV tell us. You can either *be* that friend or you can be the voice on TV that gets ignored. The call is yours. But you can't fake it. Because of the transparent nature of social media, you can't really hide who you are for long. Let's say a company pretends that they value their customers more than anything. Then they turn around and treat a customer badly. That customer has a voice. Chances are she has a Facebook profile or Twitter account. Even if she doesn't, she may tell a friend who does.

3. **People are already talking about you.** That last example tells us something else, too: people are already talking about your products, your service, and your company. It's inevitable. Social communities are breeding grounds for interaction. The only choice you have is whether you join the conversation. Every individual who interacts with your company has the potential to become a champion or a critic. You get to determine which one they become.

Two of the most powerful benefits of social media for small business are access and prominence. Tap your blog to demonstrate thought leadership (aka prominence) in your niche, and then leverage Twitter and Facebook to expand the conversation, facilitate evangelism, and grow your "following." As an example, Twitter lets you find highly relevant conversations with prospective clients, vendors, mentors, and colleagues in real time; join in, demonstrate value, and then, if appropriate, offer solutions to any problems being discussed. Do this on a regular basis and you'll grow a sizable tribe primed for your products and services.

Jonathan Fields,
author of Career Renegade

Social Media Marketing Tenets

Before we delve into the nitty-gritty of specific social media platforms and how to make the most of them, let's look at the tenets of social media marketing. These principles do not change, regardless of the technology in question.

- **Respect other people online.** Whether you're using email or instant messaging (IM) or social media: (1) don't spam people, (2) don't blindly add people to your email list, and (3) respect people's "virtual space." Basically, follow the Golden Rule; if it would annoy you, it will doubly annoy another. The same common rules of etiquette that apply offline apply online, too. Would you ever run up to someone, hand him your business card, and run away? I hope not. Yet people often do the online equivalent: post their website link—their virtual business card—blindly on people's online spaces.
- **Efforts to control or manipulate will backfire.** Did you hear the story of how the CEO of a top grocery chain got busted for pretending to be a customer and praising the company in forums? It was quite a scandal. Once his identity was

made public, it was all over. It's next to impossible to manipulate people online without getting caught. And because there are *so many* better ways to go about influencing people positively, there is no need to control the conversation.

- **Don't chase everything new under the sun.** This is a common mistake many people make when first starting out. Remember "shiny toy syndrome"? Resist the temptation to grab at everything. Do your research, pick one or two methods, and work at them consistently. This is the reason I am not covering every social media channel that's out there in this book. I've chosen instead to focus on the ones that I believe provide the highest return on investment.

- **Traffic is nice but should not be the only goal of social media marketing.** Some people out there look at social media marketing *only* as a means of attracting traffic to their websites. Although traffic is a great goal and easily measurable (it falls under Attract), it should not be your only goal. Remember, you can and should use social media to transform as well. It is a great way to share your stories, listen to feedback, and cultivate relationships with potential customers and future partners and vendors.

- **It's a good idea to use your real name.** Nine out of ten times, it's best to use your real name—even if you represent a company. Why? People don't want to be friends with McDonald's or Dell. They want to connect with others like them. We cover later when it is advisable to use your business name.

- **You have to be proactive.** This is not the same as being pushy. I hear the following a lot: "I am on Facebook and LinkedIn, but it doesn't seem to do much." My response is usually: "What exactly did you expect 'it' to do?" It's like saying you went to a networking event that didn't do anything for you. The real question here is what did *you* do at the networking event? Did you reach out to two people and have a conversation? Social media is only what you make of it.

Social Media Marketing Checklist

The following is a list of what you *must* have in place (or be in the process of putting in place) before you start with social media marketing. Remember—social media marketing is only part of the bigger picture.

- ✓ **A good BOD:** You must have a keen understanding of your brand, outcome, and differentiator.
- ✓ **A website:** Remember EMS. Your website must educate, market, and sell!
- ✓ **Content:** Ideally, your website will include a blog, because a blog makes it easy to update your site regularly with fresh content, but however you update, just make sure you do. Fresh content increases the likelihood visitors will stick around and turn into consumers.
- ✓ **An email capture mechanism:** Don't send people to your website unless you have a way to follow up with them. Ideally, this means collecting their email addresses so you can send them relevant content in the form of a newsletter or bulletin in the future.

Have all four? You're ready to rock and roll!

Visibility + Credibility = Real Social Media Success

By using social media to position yourself as an expert in your field, you'll stand out from competitors, generate buzz, and increase your value. To do this, you must market yourself as a highly visible, ideally matched source of information for your audience.

Always focus on providing valuable content, boosting your credibility, and building trust. When done correctly, you'll turn followers into loyal fans who practically do your marketing for you.

Value, credibility, and trust. Add those three things to a high level of visibility and you have the social media recipe for success.

Nancy Marmolejo,
Viva Visibility (www.VivaVisibilityBlog.com)

Which Technologies and Networks Do I Use?

Although there are thousands of social networking sites and technologies out there, in this book, I will be focusing here only on the four that I have found to be the best for marketing purposes:

- Facebook (www.facebook.com)
- Twitter (www.twitter.com)
- LinkedIn (www.linkedin.com)
- Google+ (www.plus.google.com)

I also cover certain technologies that complement social media marketing, including online video.

There's really only one way "social" and "marketing" can coexist happily. And that's if you take off your marketing hat when thinking about social media marketing and, instead, think like an average user of social media.

Allow yourself to become engrossed in the user experience on social media sites. Watch for things like how the particular "culture" of each site is constructed and maintained. Watch for things people say and do that would lead nicely into relationship building, which leads to new clients, branding, or product sales.

Since it is impossible to completely forget that you are a marketer, you will still pick up on great ways to increase business through social media, but you must think like a user first and a marketer second.

Social media users are there for anything but advertisements and pushy marketing. But make no mistake about the fact that marketing is being done successfully on these sites. It's called social marketing for a reason, and it's a very different thing that you can only see when you have your user goggles on.

Once you understand the main purpose of any social site, you can do a lot to increase your traffic and grow your business with social media in ways that don't turn off users but that engage, intrigue, and excite them.

Jack Humphrey,
FridayTrafficReport.com

For each of the four networking sites, I'll tell you:

1. Why to bother with it
2. How to use it
3. Do's and don'ts
4. Specific marketing tactics

Ready? Let's get started!

"Giving is better than receiving because giving starts the receiving process."

Jim Rohn

Identity Before Community
Why Most Companies Fail at Social Media Marketing

WHEN I WAS DOING my graduate studies in 2008 at the University of Texas at Austin, I was enamored by the world of social networking. This was a time when Twitter had just a few thousand users, and only the über-geeky were making it their playground. I was fascinated by how people pontificated on world-changing ideas in one breath (err...tweet) and shared the mundane (eating a PBJ!) in the next. I was hounded by one simple question: what compelled people to use social networking in the first place?

I theorized (as good academics are taught to do) that people craved community. They wanted to connect with each other and create communities around this very human need for connection. I was wrong. My research led me to believe that this was only a secondary reason for most social media users. The fundamental reason was that social networking sites allowed people to showcase their own identity.

Take a second to let that fully sink in. Go back and re-read that sentence, if you like. People weren't clamoring to stay connected; they wanted to, first and foremost, see their own identities reflected on the web. If most businesses and organizations looking to make a dent online truly understood this, it would change how they go about their campaigns entirely. They'd aim to put their audience's brand first rather than just push their own company brand.

Recently, I did an interview with Jeff Haden of *Inc Magazine*[1] on this very topic, and the feedback was so tremendous that I've included it here to further shine a light on this concept.

Here is some of that interview:

Jeff: You realize this premise [that identity trumps connection on social networks] is completely opposite from what most people think? Social media is supposed to be about connection, not reflection. (Sorry, couldn't resist.)

Shama: And that's why most businesses get poor results. A social site is as much a digital mirror as it is a social platform. Connection starts with understanding the meaning and impact of that reflection.

Jeff: You're going to have to explain that.

Shama: I did my graduate thesis on Twitter back when it only had only a few thousand users. My first questions were "Why would people tweet? Why would they share what they are doing?"

While I was doing the research I had this lightbulb moment. My original hypothesis was that we use social media to connect with each other, but I found the primary reason we use social media is to showcase our own identities.

Jeff: So we're all a bunch of narcissists.

Shama: It's not narcissistic at all. It's like in kindergarten (in a good way): You're having a peanut butter and jelly sandwich, and the kid next to you says he likes peanut butter and jelly,

---

[1] http://www.inc.com/jeff-haden/basic-social-media-marketing-mistake-everyone-makes.html

and then he says he likes blue crayons, and you like blue crayons...That's how we make friends and become who we are. We showcase our identities, and based on the reflection or reaction of other people, we tweak our identities.

The same is true when you're a teenager and, say, your friends like rock music. They wear certain clothes...so you do, too.

The only difference is that now all that is online. Think about Facebook profiles; Facebook really gets the idea that people, first and foremost, want to showcase who they are. Social media is like a mirror we hold up to show how we are unique and special.

It's like we're decorating the inside of our lockers again. We just transferred that to the Web.

The platforms have changed, but have the principles of how we behave and how we express ourselves? Not really.

Jeff: I get that. A friend loves to add stuff to his Facebook timeline. I tease him because he acts like a painter finishing a masterpiece. When he's done, he's a little too pleased with himself. (I know you said it's not narcissistic, but in his case I'm not so sure.)

But I'm not sure how understanding that helps a business improve its social media marketing efforts.

Shama: Here's how. Most companies still focus on the secondary aspect: getting *them* to connect with *us*. Too many companies say, "Business is about marketing and branding. We will create a brand. We will tell people who we are."

That's backward. Realizing that social media is a mirror forces companies to think not about what they want their brand to be, but what their brand says about the individual.

And that's why a cupcake shop can rack up more "likes" than a major corporation. Liking the little cupcake shop down the street says something about me as an individual: Maybe they only use organic ingredients and that's important to me. Or maybe they donate a portion of their revenue to a charity I support. In some way, that cupcake shop is a reflection of my identity and an extension of my identity brand. It reflects something I see in myself.

Liking a big company…what does that do for me? Not much. What does that say about me? Nothing.

Jeff: That's probably why I've never felt compelled to "like" a big company. (Maybe that's why I don't even have a Facebook account.)

Plus, there's the association factor. If I like a fast-food chain, I'm not going to declare it publicly. I'm not going to like an athlete's foot powder or a dandruff shampoo or adult diapers. (Not that I need any of those!) That would not only say something about me; it would say too much about me.

But I would like my local bike shop because they lead local bicycle advocacy efforts, help build new trails…and they're great guys. So liking them would say something I would feel good about saying.

Shama: For a business, what matters most is not what your brand says about you—it's what your brand says about the people you want to interact with.

The heart of building a community, whether you're a B2B or a B2C, is recognizing what that community cares about. It's not manipulative; it's not sneaky—it's the most authentic way to brand your business and grow a following online.

It's not manipulative because it's about what you do, not what you say. It's about what you do and what that says about the people who like you for doing it.

Jeff: I see and hear stuff like "Like us on Facebook!" or "Follow us on Twitter!" all over the place, and I always wonder what the business is thinking. Why would I? You haven't given me a reason.

And I'm immediately turned off when I have to "like" a business to get a discount or special offer. But maybe that's just me.

I wouldn't feel a connection to the company. It would just be a transaction. "Here's my like, now give me my discount."

Shama: There's a much better approach that doesn't require incentives or promotions. (Although there is nothing wrong with either.)

I was speaking at a real estate conference and a number of people said they were frustrated because they had created social media platforms for their real estate businesses and nothing was happening. The problem was they had sites . . . but those sites didn't say anything about the people they wanted to engage.

But if they changed their focus and created a site like, say, "Why Dallas Rocks," and it was powered by Dallas Realtors . . . Then you can get "likes" because it says a lot about me: I like my city, I like my community . . . and I like you for getting that.

The same is true for a wedding site. Say you sell bridal gowns—how many people are going to follow you? Change the focus. Create a site like "All About Brides," or "I Can't Believe I'm Engaged," or "OMG I'm Engaged!" . . . powered by Downtown Bridal.

Which will get more likes? The site focused on showing people what you are, or the site focused on how brides feel about themselves? Brides will want to connect with you when they know you get *them.*

Jeff: But what if I'm in a service business? What if my business isn't so much about products but about, for want of a better way to put it, me?

Shama: The same principle applies; in fact, when people are the focus it can be even more powerful.

That's why letting people connect with the CEO works so well. It's an extension of your brand. It's a relationship. Who would you rather connect with, a company or a person?

And that's why I resisted creating a page for our agency for a long time. I finally caved in when we decided to use it for customer service and answering questions. But it proves my point: I have over 200K Facebook subscribers, and our agency page has a few thousand. People like being able to connect with the CEO.

People want to connect with people. When you connect with a person at a business, it's like you know someone there. That's really powerful.

Jeff: Now put it into action. Tell me what to do.

Shama: The key is to forget what you want to say about yourself. Think about what your customers want to say and feel about themselves.

1. Start with your customers.

Forget *your* brand. What do your *customers* see as their brand?

Forget *your* messaging. What is the messaging of your *audience*?

For example, there's an Italian restaurant nearby. The interior is splashed with pictures of the owners, their families, and generations of people who have eaten there. They encourage customers to put their pictures up. When you walk in you instantly know they care about family, about tradition…you can tell family means everything to them.

People who care about family connect with the restaurant because it says something about how they see themselves.

Think in broader terms. How do your customers see themselves? What is important to them?

2. Create a platform that integrates your customers' brand with what you offer.

One of our clients runs chiropractic clinics. Many of their patients were injured in accidents. So they built a "don't text and drive" platform. They've created an entire campaign around preventing accidents. They frequently speak at schools and community events. They even created a pledge people can feature on their profiles to show it's something they care about. It's like bumper stickers on steroids.

The community cares about protecting their kids and, be honest, adults, because everyone is guilty of texting while they're driving. Our client cares about it, too. And they prove it.

Or take American Express: who would join a social network for a credit card company? No one. So Amex built Open Forum and created a community for small-business people who need information and resources. They do crazy numbers. If a credit card company can do it...you can too.

Determine what you stand for, blend that with what your customers care about, and find the right balance point.

3. Be part of a movement.

Marketing has always been about you: your needs and your objectives.

Of course the goal is to get leads and sales, but with social media you should look at something bigger, become a part of a movement...be part of something your audience cares about.

Then you get more than bottom-line results: you get to be a part of something bigger and more meaningful.

The Dallas YMCA did a campaign featuring stories about their members and how the Y changed their life. In effect, they created a collage of beautiful stories and pictures. Those stories mean something to people. We all want to change our lives for the better and to be around people who feel the same way.

Bottom line: Don't mistake the medium for the message. That's not what it is.

Find a way to be of service—and to be a part of something bigger than your business.

> "Facebook is a platform, a medium, and a killer app. It's contagious, infectious, and viral—but in the best meaning of those words."
>
> Elliot Schrage,
> *Facebook.com*

Facebook

With 950 Million Users and Growing, This Giant Can't Be Ignored

Why Bother with Facebook?

- Facebook has more than 950 million *active* users, and it's growing every day.
- More than half log on at least once a day.
- More than half are out of college.
- Its fastest-growing demographic is those twenty-five years old and older.
- It offers fantastic online visibility for your brand.
- People are talking about you on there anyway. You may as well join in the conversation!

Facebook is like a coffee shop. Everyone is there for his or her own reasons, but it is a great place to strike up a conversation.

People from all walks of life use Facebook. They aren't there to buy stuff. They are there, first and foremost, to express themselves. After self-expression comes their need to connect with others.

Research shows that people use Facebook primarily to show-case their own identity—not just who they are but who they want to be perceived as. The friends we make, the groups we join, and the pages we "like" on Facebook are all offshoots of this basic identity creation and re-creation.

This is why you can never push products or services on Face-book. If you try to convert people directly to customers or clients, you will fail. However, if you are looking to attract consumers and build relationships over time, you will succeed. Your goal on Face-book should always be to attract people to your website, build trust, and gain visibility—all things that inevitably lead to sales.

AHA! Zen Moment

Think about how you can be a part of people's identity. Remember the cool kid everyone wanted to be friends with in school? Why did everyone want to be that person's friend? Because it meant he or she was cool, too! You want to position your brand so people want to make it part of their identity. 🧘

How to Use Facebook

Facebook can be divided into five main parts: profiles (now also called timelines), pages, groups, events, and ads. Each part serves a certain function, and each has to be used uniquely.

Your profile is a way for you to present yourself to others. The main page of your profile is your own unique timeline. Over time, that timeline is populated by your life events, as well as a selection of updates and wall posts, organized by year. You can-not share a timeline.

Pages, short for fan pages, are for essentially anything and anyone that someone would care to be a fan of. Everything from Oreos to rock bands can have a page. Businesses and other en-tities have pages, not profiles, though pages also now use the timeline format.

Groups allow people to create subcommunities within Facebook around a topic of interest. There are serious groups, such as "Entrepreneurship," and silly ones like "I know what you did last summer."

Facebook events can be set up to attract participants to any live or virtual event.

Facebook advertising allows you to reach your target market based on their demographics and interests.

Facebook has gone from being just a social network for college students to a social center for people and businesses from all walks of life, and it has had to evolve to keep up. But although Facebook is constantly changing to keep up with demand, a lot of the basics remain the same.

Your Facebook Profile

This is where it all begins. Your Facebook profile is your personal space, your billboard, your calling card! A profile is *not* for businesses. A Facebook profile is for individuals only. Your profile is created automatically when you sign up for a Facebook account, and you will need a profile in order to join groups, add friends, generate ads, and create events.

If you are marketing your personal brand and don't mind the overlap of professional and personal, you can use your profile as a branding marketing tool. If you are marketing a business or a brand that you wish to keep separate from your personal network, you will want to focus on building a fan page. You can use your profile or your fan page (as we'll discuss later) to ATTRACT people initially, as well as intrigue them enough to visit your website (off of Facebook). You attract them by showcasing your expertise and sharing value.

To make sure you understand how to make the *most* of your Facebook profile, I use my own profile as an example. Just keep in mind that Facebook pages have become much more robust than profiles over time in terms of marketing. We will get to them soon!

Status Updates (Your Timeline)

When you log in to Facebook, you are asked: "What's on your mind?" This is a very tricky question, because—let's face it—lots of thoughts run through our minds, and if we shared all of them, it would create a lot of noise. No one really cares if you just had breakfast, are getting an oil change, or just dropped off your kids at school.

Use the status updates in a strategic way. Share important business news, announce events, give advice, and provide *value*. Status updates are really the heart of Facebook because they create an ongoing impression of the person posting them. "Oh, Joe—he is such a partier. Just look at his Facebook updates!" "Jane—she is such a giver! She is constantly sharing tips with us." Share only when what you are doing matches your brand and provides value. In the following example, I mention that I am finishing up my book. This reminds people that I am writing a book; it builds curiosity! Plus, it's good information for anyone awaiting its release to have.

 Shama is putting the finishing touches on her book! a moment ago - clear

What are you doing right now?

Status updates are also great for starting conversations. You (and your friends) have the ability to comment on any status you post. It's a quick way to build stronger relationships.

As an attempt to keep up with Google+ and improve their privacy settings, Facebook has changed this update feature significantly. You can now tag your friends, include your location, and determine exactly who sees the individual updates that you make. Once you click the update bar, you will see these features pictured here.

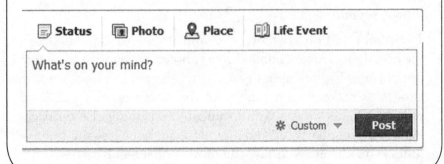

Facebook now allows you to highlight your status updates on your timeline. This means your status will be featured across the top of your timeline when people visit that page.

The following three stories illustrate how I have leveraged Facebook, using status updates and Notes, to further my business.

1. **Snagged a speaking engagement**: I posted that I was speaking at a local Dallas–Fort Worth event on Facebook marketing. Another local, Elizabeth Marshall, caught the update and asked if I was willing to speak to her group on the same topic. I said yes, and we soon discovered that we were alums of the same high school—and even shared a favorite teacher! Liz and I have gone on to become good friends and have partnered on many occasions since.

2. **Received a press opportunity**: One day I got a phone call from a local TV station. They were doing a segment on Facebook and wanted to interview me. How did they know about me? A reporter from Austin had seen my updates on Facebook and knew I spoke on the topic. She'd given them my name.

3. **Established expertise**: When we succeeded in getting one of our client's keywords in the Google top ten, I posted an update about it. It was a great way to showcase our work because it established our expertise in the area and reminded people of what we can do. It also showcased my genuine excitement over our results.

About Section

The About section is where you want to showcase yourself in the best light. This section has five subsections: work and education, history by year, about you, living, and contact info. You can choose to make certain aspects of the About section public or private. Whereas users tend to update everything else on Facebook fairly regularly, this area remains more or less the same—unless you change your favorite movies on a regular basis!

Fill out your About section as professionally and purposefully as possible. I can't stress this enough. Even though this is your personal profile, people will judge you professionally by it. This doesn't mean you can't have a life. By all means, share your interests and hobbies—but don't share anything that you wouldn't share with a stranger on the street.

Your profile information should be entered with a purpose in mind and reflect important events throughout your life—your life story. Are you going to use Facebook to attract more people to your business or are you going to use it to attract your next job? What do you want someone to walk away with after looking at your profile?

Did you know that lawyers can look up your Facebook profile and use it to *judge* whether you should be on a jury? Yes, the information you put up on Facebook can be used as evidence in a court of law. Furthermore, the FTC has ruled that companies can screen job applicants based on their internet photos and postings (that's everything from Facebook and Twitter to Flickr and blogs). In essence, what you decide to put online could determine your future.

Given that, you should fill out your About section as professionally as possible—even if you don't plan on using your personal profile for business. And don't share anything you would be embarrassed to find made public.

Facebook News Feed

Although not part of your profile, your Facebook News Feed is unique to you and is the first thing you see when you log in to your account. It is the center column of your Facebook home page, and it constantly refreshes with a stream of updates (including links, pictures, and videos) from your Facebook friends and pages you like or subscribe to. Most people on Facebook don't visit profiles of their friends or visit the pages they like on a regular basis. They depend solely on the news feed. To manage the updates you're subscribed to, go to a friend's timeline and move your cursor over the Friends button at the top of the timeline. Select "Show in News Feed" to turn updates on or off.

Your Facebook feed is sorted into two different types of stories: Top Stories and Most Recent News. Facebook defaults to showing all Top Stories since your last visit at the top of your news feed. Depending on the number of friends you have and how often you check Facebook, sometimes you may not have any Top Stories. It also shows you a link that lets you jump to Most Recent News, which features the latest updates from your friends in a reverse chronological order. How does Facebook determine Top Stories? It bases it on an algorithm, much like Google or any other search engine does for search results. It uses factors such as how many of your friends commented on a story, who posted the story, what type of story it is (photo, video, or status update), and how much you interact with a particular friend or page. In addition to posts from friends and pages you follow, you will see tags, friend requests, event updates, group memberships, and other items reflecting your friends' Facebook activity. In short, it shows you news on what it calculates as being relevant to you rather than just what's recent. There's also a newly introduced ticker on the side of the page, which shows you what your friends are commenting on in real time.

If the marketer in you is wondering, "So, how can we end up on people's news feeds more?" that's an excellent question, and we will cover it momentarily. For now, I just want to make sure you're familiar with this terminology and setup.

Here is what my news feed looks like as I'm writing this:

Facebook Privacy Settings

Facebook has created some very robust privacy settings, allowing you to decide who gets to view what part of your Facebook presence. For example, you may allow everyone to see your basic profile but only a select few to see your pictures. You can control those privacy settings by choosing Settings and then Privacy Settings from the top menu bar. And as discussed previously, you can adjust the settings on individual status updates as well. The privacy settings control only general information; for everything else you can choose your audience each time you post.

A word of caution here: although you can certainly make things private, nothing is 100 percent secure. Facebook, after all, is just a website. It can experience glitches. If a glitch occurs and your private information is made public, make sure it isn't anything that would cause you embarrassment. Also keep in mind that your Facebook friends may share your information with others—intentionally or unintentionally. I personally know many people who let others, such as bosses or spouses, use their account to browse Facebook.

Again, never share anything—publicly or privately—that you wouldn't be comfortable sharing with a complete stranger.

How to Build Your Facebook Friendship Base

Does the number of friends you have matter? Yes, to a degree. Does this mean you should obsess over building your numbers? No. Having more friends is great because it means you have a bigger pool to network with. You can use Facebook to keep up with current customers and vendors, and you can also use it to meet new people. But a lot of people get stuck on the word "friends" and equate their friend number with their worth. It totally depends on how you wish to define a "Facebook friend." Remember that on Facebook, "friend" may just mean someone you know.

Facebook now allows people to subscribe to your updates rather than be your friend. It also allows people who subscribe to you to repost your update to their own network, beyond your friends and subscribers. When they repost, subscribers help spread your personal and professional brand.

You do want to focus on having a high-quality group to network with. Let's look at four ways you can start building a quality base of both friends and subscribers.

1. **Use the tools that Facebook provides when you first create an account.** One tool will look through your email address book to see who in it is already using Facebook. This is a quick way to find people you already know. You can send a friend request to anyone you want, but start with good friends and colleagues so you can start to build your network fast. Also, don't be surprised if the first time you log on, you see friend requests waiting for you to approve. More people than you realize may already be on Facebook and looking for you!
2. **Bring offline networking online.** When you go to conferences or mixers and bring home a stack of business cards, search for those people on Facebook and add them as friends. Then throw away their cards! Facebook will even remind you of their birthdays.

Marketing with social media has created an equal, level playing field for this new era in business. It has given personal brands an opportunity to compete with big brands. Entrepreneurs don't have to have a big budget or a lot of capital to position themselves as a thought leader in their industry. As someone who started without a big following, database, or big budget, marketing with social media gave me the chance to position myself as an authority in the marketing arena. Now anyone with a passion and a message can do the same thing and build a loyal tribe.

Alejandro Reyes,
Successfool.com

3. **Register your Facebook username**. Facebook allows each profile to have an easy username and custom URL. You can go to www.facebook.com/username to set up your own username. This makes it very easy for you to share your profile with others.

4. **Allow subscribers**. From your personal timeline, click the subscribers tab on the left menu, underneath the cover photo. This will allow you to post public updates and allow people outside of your network of friends to read them. Your subscribers will see only the updates that you make public. If you wish to share something only with friends, you can.

Facebook Groups

Facebook groups work really well for currently existing offline or other online groups. For example, you can set up a group for your company, your college reunion planning committee, or even your CEO breakfast group. You can keep your group open to the public, closed (anyone can see that the group exists if they search for it, but only members can access and see posts), or even secret (invite-only and can't be found in searches). Groups don't work so well when you are trying to market a product or build brand awareness. Do not create a group around your brand or business. This is what (as we will soon discuss) pages are for.

Groups are very much like online forums. Forums are a modern equivalent of a traditional bulletin board: a place where users generate content, host discussions, and create a community of sorts. On Facebook, the owner of a group serves as its moderator.

They are a fabulous way to create your community for free. You can find groups by clicking on the Groups icon (on the left side of the bottom menu bar). You can go to www.facebook.com/groups to search and create groups. You can also invite friends to join your group. A person doesn't have to be your Facebook friend to join your group, but you can (and should) invite friends you think would be interested to join. You don't want to invite people blindly, however. Let's say you want to set up a Facebook group for your son's school's PTA. You want to specifically invite those friends whom you know are part of the PTA. There is one huge drawback of groups—less for the creator and more for the members. It works based on an opt-out system versus an opt-in one. That means you can add any friend to a group; he or she doesn't have to give you consent first. Then, if that friend chooses not be a part of it, he or she can leave—an opt-out system. Facebook may change this eventually. For now, you want to be careful when you add people to a group. Be sure that you have their consent or know that they would truly want to be a part of the group before you add them.

On the following page is a group that I belong to—offline and online. It is called the Young Entrepreneur Council, and it's made up of young entrepreneurs who support each other in their ventures and work to reduce youth unemployment.

What all can you do with Facebook groups?

- Connect and network with other like-minded individuals.
- Provide a convenient place for your current network to meet and stay connected.
- Provide value and increase visibility within your current group.

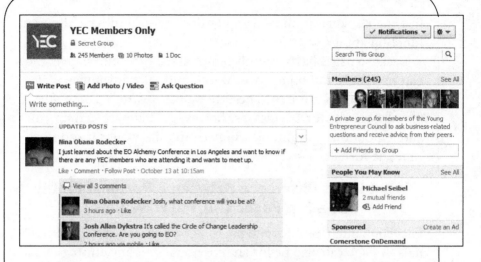

- Post relevant pictures and videos. This provides content as well as helps your group members feel like they are part of the community.

Facebook Pages

Facebook pages, or fan pages, as they are sometimes called, were created in late 2007 because Facebook wanted to give businesses a space for their brands but didn't want businesses to create profiles, which Facebook reserved for people. If Facebook finds that a business has created a profile instead of a page, they will close the account. This is why you should keep your profiles personal and create a *page* for your business.

Pages are much more customizable than groups, and you can have an unlimited number of "likes" The best part is that pages are indexed by Google. By default, all fan pages are public. That means if someone searches for your company or for keywords that you cover in your page, your page will show up in Google's search results. This is an easy step toward search engine optimization.

If you are looking to build a brand and market your company, you will want a fan page, hands down. You will notice that fan pages have switched over to the timeline format, much like the personal profiles. Despite this, pages still have different functions/uses.

Because pages have recently adopted the timeline change, they can now have a unique cover photo and take advantage of several other new features. These new features may come with a few drawbacks for businesses, however. There are certain rules and regulations your brand will need to follow once it adopts the timeline format.

What Is the Difference Between a Personal Profile and a Fan Page? Can You Have Both?

Facebook offers profiles and pages. A profile is meant for individuals. A page can also be for an individual, but any entity (a business, a nonprofit, a dog) can also setup a page. The original idea was that profiles allowed you to connect with people you knew, like your friends, while a page allowed you to connect with a greater audience. Anyone who wanted to get your updates could "like" a page. However, with the launch of the timeline feature, Facebook also added a new feature to personal profiles—the Subscribe feature. Now, if you allow it, people can subscribe to your profile. Anyone who subscribes to your profile can see anything that you have made public. And your information shows up in their Facebook news feeds. Subscribing and friending are exclusive of each other. You can subscribe to someone's profile without becoming their friend. And even if you friend someone on Facebook, you can unsubscribe to their updates.

The question becomes: do you now need both—a profile and a page? If your company wants a presence on Facebook, a page is still the best option. However, if you are an individual, you can choose to have a profile, which allows subscribers versus having a page. The upside to this is that you have to manage only one account. The downside is that you cannot market or advertise to your subscribers like you can to fans of your page. At least not yet. In order to save time and increase efficiency, I dropped my personal fan page and instead allowed the subscriber option on my profile. As of writing this, I have 239,000 subscribers. The tough part is that I don't have any special mechanism (like Face-book advertising) to reach all my subscribers the way I used to. At any given time, I reach only those who see my information in their news feed.

The Marketing Zen Group has a page, as well. I resisted creating this officially for a long time. As the CEO, I wanted people to be able to connect with me personally. However, people started "liking" The Marketing Zen Group without us even setting up a page for it. After 50 likes, it was obvious that the people had spoken. They wanted us to have a presence on Facebook. So we "claimed" the company, and now have an official company fan page as well. You can visit it at www.facebook.com/MarketingZenGroup.

Here is my personal profile:

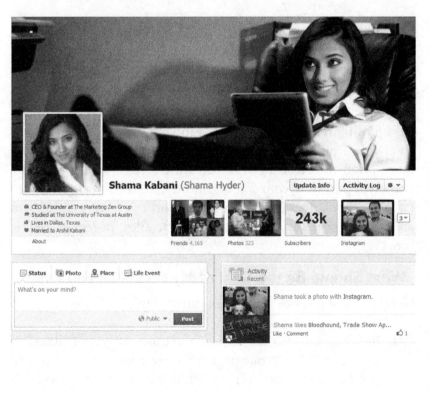

Here is our company's fan page:

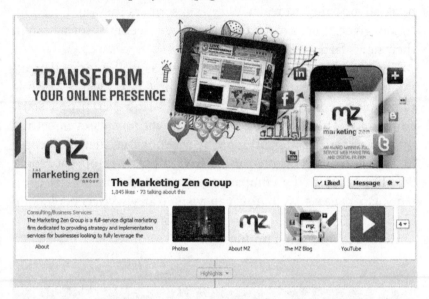

What If I Already Have a Profile for My Business with a Large Following?

Not to worry—Facebook has a tool that will convert your business profile to a page for you! Go to www.facebook.com/pages/create.php?migrate and you can complete the transition. You will go through the basic steps for creating a page, and then Facebook will port over your photos and transform your friends into fans. Facebook does not currently support converting a profile to an existing page or merging multiple profiles, pages, or places, however.

What Should Be the Goal of My Facebook Fan Page?

Ideally, you should be focused on three things:

1. **Building up your fan base**. This comes by way of "likes." If someone "likes" your page, they are considered a fan. Did you know that the average annualized value of a Facebook fan is $136.38? That number includes product spending,

brand loyalty, propensity to recommend, and many other factors (which vary by industry).

2. **Keeping interaction consistent and high**. A study of over 4,000 pages by AllFacebook.com revealed that only 17 percent of fans see an average post. Why? They don't show up in their news feeds. And the key to landing in people's news feeds is eliciting fan interaction (comments, likes) on your posts. You can now use the "promote post" tool, which costs between $5 and $300 per use, to make sure more of your fans see your post. Aside from this, you can also pin and highlight important posts. Also worth noting: some kinds of posts naturally receive more interaction than others. Photo albums, pictures, and videos receive 180 percent, 120 percent, and 100 percent more engagement respectively.

3. **Driving traffic and leads to your website**. Remember, Facebook is a tool to attract!

How to Promote Your Facebook Page

You should be using every tool in your toolbox to promote your Facebook page at its inception (and throughout your entire social media journey).

Hit the Ground Running

Begin by sending a designated email blast to the current clients in your email database. Send an internal email instructing employees to like your page and recommend the page to their friends and family members.

To do so, they go to your Facebook page, click the Settings icon next to the "Message" button, and scroll down to click "Share." Employ your current customers as your brand ambassadors and ask them to help spread the word about your new page.

You can select a username for your page, just like you can for your personal profile. To do this, follow the same instructions given in the profile section of this chapter. Make sure to check your spelling because you can edit it only once after it is created!

If you have a physical location associated with your brand (or multiple franchises, offices, etc.), use traditional signage to notify customers that you are joining the Facebook world. Incorporate QR codes into the creative design on each poster or tabletop to connect instantly with smartphone users.

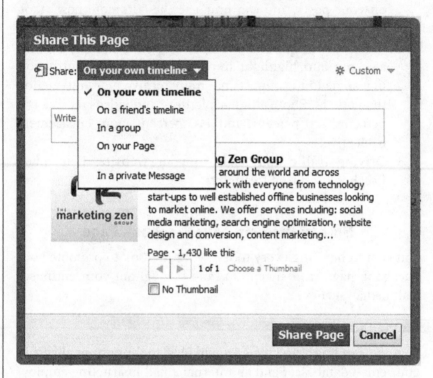

You can also set your business up as a place and offer exclusive items to consumers when they check in to encourage them to connect with you. The best part? You get free social advertising when the update is sent out to their Facebook friends that they checked in at your page!

To set up your place on Facebook, you must be at your physical location. On a smartphone, go to Facebook Places. Click "Check in" and search for your listing (a customer may have already set it up, in which case you can search for it on Facebook and click "Claim my business" at the bottom). If you cannot find it, click "Add new" and fill out the details. When you add your correct address to your Facebook page, the two will automatically sync up.

Once you get to 200 fans, you cannot change your page name, so make sure your choice is well thought out!

Posting Basics

Beyond that, having a firm social media policy and/or guidelines in place helps to keep posting orderly, approved, and representing your brand appropriately. What to post on your fan page—and when and how—depends on your brand and company. It also depends on how your customers want to interact with you, which is the most important thing.

―――――― AHA! Zen Moment ――――――

POSTING Q&A

From a report in Momentous Media:

1. *What is the best time to post?*
   answer: Weekends and off-peak hours
2. *How many times should I post per day?*
   answer: As many times as you want
3. *What type of content elicits the most interaction?*
   answer: #1 Photos, #2 Statuses
4. *Should I ask fans to Like and Comment on my posts?*
   answer: Yes! Asking to Like increases interaction 216 percent
5. *Should I ask my fans questions?*
   answer: Questions don't increase the interaction rate, but they do increase commenting rate. Make sure to ask fans to answer your questions with a comment.

6. *How long should my status messages be?*
   answer: Long or short, we found no correlation between length and interaction rate.
7. *How long do my posts last in the Newsfeed?*
   answer: As of 2010, fifty percent of clicks happened within one hour; ninety percent happen within nine hours. 🧘

Don't be afraid to step outside of the box with your posting. If you post a link every day to your website (unless you have a very dynamic, robust site), your audience is going to get bored. There is nothing wrong with posting about current events; in fact, most times they spark more interaction. Just be careful not to impose your own opinion. For instance, baked goods company Entenmann's faced backlash on Twitter when they used the #notguilty hashtag made popular by the Casey Anthony trial. A Twitter uproar started, and Entenmann's was very quick to apologize, admitting they didn't know what the hashtag referenced. The same goes for Facebook. Be mindful of what you are saying, what you are posting, and what your audience may say or do in response.

Here are a few ideas for content generation:

- Blog posts
- Quotes (people love to "like" quotes)
- Questions about people's lives
- Questions about holiday plans
- Exciting company breakthroughs/happenings
- Employee spotlights or anything personal (especially with larger brands where people aren't expecting this type of transparency—surprise them!)
- Comments on current events
- Articles related to your industry
- Funny facts related to your product or service
- Shout-outs to communities your brand interacts with
- Local or national stories of goodwill
- Videos and photos

Facebook Questions is a great feature for pages to use. As the newer addition to the status bar on your page, Questions allows people to (1) have defined answers, (2) share the poll with their friends, (3) keep a record on their profile of the questions they have answered, and (4) add their own options to maintain a sense of personalization.

Using Timeline to Promote Your Brand

There are several features that come with the new timeline format that are useful for promotion—especially since the timeline is the first thing new visitors see.

1. **Pin your post**. You can now pin important posts to the top of your timeline for up to seven days. (You can do this up to three days after the original post is made.)
2. **Highlight stories**. You can highlight important stories/ events on your timeline by starring them in the right-hand corner of the post.
3. **Set brand milestones**. For example, launching a new product, winning awards, or opening a new store. Don't limit yourself to current milestones; with the timeline feature you can go back and add milestones to the company history. These appear highlighted on your timeline.
4. **Add a unique cover photo**. Your cover photo is a great way to help your fans visualize your brand. There are, however, limitations. You cannot include purchase info or sales, contact information (website, address, phone), or calls to action ("like us," "get it now").
5. **Promote your post**. Promoting your posts increases the number of fans who see it in their news feed. Each post has it's own set of analytics, called "insights," that allows you to see how many fans it reached.

Campaigns and Contests

We encourage our clients to launch some sort of campaign or contest relating to their brand in an effort to draw in new fans and to keep current fans coming back to the page to connect. Offer all your fans a discount of some sort, offer a free product or service, or give away a fun new piece of technology. Larger or more exclusive prizes yield higher entrance rates, but try to use something that relates to your brand.

The less information or work that is required on the entrant's part, the more likely people are to actually enter. Be sure to collect an email address (so that you can contact the winner), but if you intend to use it for anything else, you must notify entrants. Also, be sure to have an extensive list of rules (you can put this in your notes section on your page) outlining your rights to use their submitted content, age requirements, state laws, or whatever applies to your campaign.

Here are a few ways to share your contest or campaign:

- Use Facebook Advertising (see Chapter 9)
- Reach out to bloggers in your industry to help spread the word
- Send a designated email blast to your current database
- Share the contest on Twitter, YouTube, and any other channels your brand uses
- Post signage about the campaign at your physical location
- Promote your contest posts to encourage maximum visibility within your current network
- Have staff personally encourage clients to enter

Be prepared to lose a few fans at the end of your contest, as "like 'em and leave 'em" Facebook users do exist. And if you have a campaign in which you select a winner personally, be prepared for user backlash. Though you may not always have to combat this, contests where users select a winner or where one is chosen at random leave less room for speculation about playing favorites or fixed results.

Most important, be sure to read up on Facebook's ever-changing promotions guidelines to make sure your contest complies (Facebook has the power to ban certain pages because of non-compliance). Watch for updates here: www.facebook.com/ promotions_guidelines.php.

Facebook Events

Facebook's events are a great way to promote any event or milestone, and also provide a channel for direct communication with your fans through event "attendance." It doesn't even have to be a physical event. Virtual events like teleseminars, webinars, and even reminders to enter a contest also qualify.

When you create a Facebook event, you get a full page featuring your event (which looks much like a group or page).

As it does with pages, Facebook allows indexing of public events. This means SEO benefits for you! You can choose to show the attendees or not, make the event public or private, and customize your message entirely.

What kinds of events can you promote?

- Local live events
- Live events in other cities
- Contests/campaigns
- Performances
- Book signings
- Teleseminars/webinars
- Virtual events
- Product launches
- New store openings
- Nonprofit events (walks, benefits, etc.)
- Parties
- Educational classes
- Meetings (formal or informal)

How to Create an Event on Facebook

Go to your brand's Facebook page, click on the events tab under the profile picture, and click "Create an Event." You will be presented with a simple form, like the one on the next page, to fill out. Note that you can host an event personally or host through a group you moderate.

Keys to Promoting Your Event on Facebook

Follow these seven guidelines:

1. **Choose a catchy title.** I get at least five event requests a day. I look at only the ones that catch my eye.
2. **Create a clear and thorough description.** It's annoying to see one-liners. "Join Us" isn't a description. Show people what's in it for them.

3. **Include time zones.** Facebook has users on every continent—including Antarctica. Remember to select the appropriate time zone in the description area.

4. **Invite your guests to bring their friends.** You want to get the word out, right? Encourage your friends to invite other friends. But...

5. **Don't invite blindly.** Spend some time thinking about who might benefit by attending. Add this to your description: "You are being invited because..." Also, note that you can no longer invite fans from the page itself. You can only post the event on the timeline. Admins must invite using their personal accounts.

6. **Post pictures and video.** Did you host the same event last year? Share those pictures! Give people something that will help them get a feel for the event.

About Facebook Applications

Ever been bitten by a zombie or been invited to a Mafia wars game? Ever raised virtual farm animals on Facebook? If so, you've interacted with an application, or "app" as they are better known. Applications are also what allow you to take quizzes like "Which *Friends* Character Are You?" As Facebook evolves, Facebook applications will continue to gain popularity and visibility. Most applications aren't developed by Facebook but by outside companies.

Can You Use Applications as a Marketing Tool?

Yes! Applications are a great way for brands to interact and give back to their fans, especially if it has a very specific tie-in to the product. This Dunkin' Donuts app is very popular because when people connect to it in order to play a game, their points go toward their Dunkin' purchases.

One fairly successful application is the Schweppes "Profile App," which allows users to take one image and crop it to fit across their five photo series. I used this and at least fifty people asked me about it and ended up using it within the first week.

Facebook now requires pages to host contests on third-party applications such as Shortstack, OfferPop, or Wildfire (see more that follows). Once activated, these applications are then featured under your page's main profile image. They are easy to share and can support any feature of your contest or campaign. Refer to the Campaigns and Contests section for more information.

What About Adding Applications on Your Page?

Each brand and industry benefits from different apps. An art gallery may benefit from simple Facebook apps like Photos and Videos, whereas a restaurant chain may benefit from a personalized online ordering application. You can edit what apps are visible on your timeline by clicking on the right-hand corner of each one under the cover photo. By then clicking the pencil icon, you can swap positions, edit the app, or remove it.

If you're considering creating an app, the trick is to make one that is enticing enough that users will be willing to connect with it, thereby relinquishing their personal information. As your app becomes an important part of how users express themselves, their app-related actions are more prominently displayed throughout timeline, news feed, and ticker, thus reaching their friend network and giving your company more visibility.

A directory of applications can be found at www.facebook.com/apps.

About Facebook Ads

Because Facebook is teeming with people, it would seem to make sense that Facebook ads should be a great investment; however, Facebook ads still have a long way to go. People on Facebook aren't in shopping mode yet. They aren't even searching for information (as they might be while searching Google). They are looking to connect with their friends, update their profiles, and just stay current. What this means is that they are happy playing in the Facebook sandbox; they don't want to go outside Facebook

Marketers need to be where their customers and potential customers are, and increasingly, this is on social networking sites. Social networks are emerging as a powerful and sophisticated new kind of marketing channel. Marketing is becoming precise, personal, and social: social networking sites are giving marketers new abilities to hyper-target campaigns using profile information, engage community members by tapping into social capital within friend groups, and systematically cultivate word-of-mouth marketing across their existing customer base. For many products and services, recommendations and referrals from trusted friends and colleagues are important factors in deciding whether to buy.

From The Facebook Era: Tapping Online Social Networks to Build Better Products, Reach New Audiences, and Sell More Stuff *by Clara Shih (@clarashih on Twitter), who developed the first business application on Facebook and is currently CEO of Hearsay Labs*

to another site. However, ads can be used successfully to market Facebook groups and pages. Even if people don't click on the ads, you still get increased visibility when they appear.

With Facebook's ability to target so specifically, the question has become, "Are these ads creepy, or do users like being shown only that which they want to see?"

The following information comes from one of The Marketing Zen Group's clients, Beverly Hills Aesthetics (BHA). The ad campaign pertained to a "Pucker Up" promotion they ran, in which the participants had to guess how many "kisses" there were in the jar at the front desk of the office. The winner would receive a $100 gift certificate to be used toward any service. We used Facebook ads to promote this contest for our client.

BHA's goal was to use Facebook advertising to increase their Pucker Up entrants as well as attract new patients by promoting their services. Their Facebook page served as the primary source of information about the contest; it was where the Facebook ad linked. We also posted specials, prices, relevant articles, brand information, pictures, and videos on their wall, and fans of the page could post and comment there, too.

We chose to target females thirty-two to sixty-five years old who lived within 50 miles of LA. The ad they ran had two lifetimes: the first ran from June 2011 to July 2011, and the second ran from July 2011 to August 2011. The advertising budget was $1,200 per month.

BHA found tremendous success with this promotional campaign. In total, their ad had more than 4.5 million impressions and garnered 1,696 clicks. Their average cost per click was $0.68. As a result of the boost in exposure, the office also saw an increase in online leads and in office calls.

The following are tips for advertising on Facebook:

- **Identify your goal.** What do you specifically want to do? For BHA, it was to increase appointments and online leads in the hopes it would result in an increase in overall revenue from June to October 2011. (It did!)

- **Be specific in segment targeting.** For BHA, we targeted locations relevant to their business. Given that the office is located in Beverly Hills, we targeted that city. We also targeted adults thirty-two to sixty-five years old, because that is the most popular demographic for office procedures. (You can now target Facebook ads by zip code and by a city's surrounding areas.)
- **Use keyword targeting.** You can take targeting a step further by allowing your ad to appear only to people whose profiles use certain keywords. For example, next time BHA could target their ad to people whose profiles mention words or phrases such as "cellulite," "liposuction," "cosmetic surgery," and "plastic surgery Beverly Hills." You can target specific terms like these, or use broader categories like "beauty," "health," and "plastic surgery."
- **Make the ad clear, concise, and simple.** Ours read:

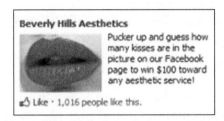

- **Use a call to action.** Encourage the viewer to click the advertisement. For BHA, the call to action was "Pucker up and guess how many kisses are in the picture on our Facebook page to win $100 toward any aesthetic service!" More specific phrases such as "Like us to learn more about _____" have been proven quite effective as well.

We have run very successful campaigns for other clients as well. Although Facebook is relatively new, it has been proven to be far more successful than Google AdWords pay-per-click marketing in local markets.

Some other Facebook Advertising tips to remember:

- Change content and creative frequently (about once a week) to keep your ads fresh for viewers who will see them repeatedly.
- The CPC (cost per click) method has proven much more cost-effective than the CPM (cost per thousand) model, which is based on impressions.
- You can share your account activity with colleagues or clients by going to "Ads," then "Settings," and adding permissions. Never leave these unattended. This is your money hard at work, so watch your bids, your budget, and your overall performance to get the most bang for your buck.
- People respond well to smiling women. When in doubt, make your ad image a smiling woman!
- Check all your links, landing pages, and applications before beginning your campaign.
- Experiment with different types of ads (sponsored stories, ads that link directly to your page, ads that link to an external page, customized titles, etc.) and see what works for you.

Did you know that if you spend a certain amount each month in advertising (currently $5,000) that you qualify for the Facebook Fast Track Program and can receive help from a specific Facebook ads account executive? Through this program, you receive hands-on guidance from this account executive to make the most of your ad campaign. If you work with an agency, they may already have a Facebook account executive who provides insight on their clients' accounts. Once you get close to spending $5,000 on Facebook Advertising, they will send you an email regarding this program.

Facebook Open Graph

Facebook Connect is being replaced by Open Graph as a means for sharing web content while being connected to your personal profile. Just as Facebook Connect allowed users to "like" certain content or comment on blogs as their Facebook profile and share the activity on their wall, Open Graph aims to make all web content "likeable," "shareable," and available for commenting. After a user adds the app, app-specific actions are shared on Facebook via Open Graph.

In short, Open Graph allows users to "connect" their Facebook identity, friends, and settings to any website. If you have ever commented on a blog, you probably had to provide your name, email address, and website URL. Now if a website has Facebook Open Graph in place, you can simply log in to the website using your Facebook ID. As a website owner, you definitely want to have Facebook Open Graph set up on your website. It takes some technical savvy, but you can find all the directions at developers.facebook.com/docs/opengraph. Now, not only can visitors to your website log in using their Facebook ID, but you can see exactly who is visiting your website. And when they comment on your blog, it shows on their profile for all their friends to see as well. This means that as a brand all your products and services will have that much more of a chance of being recognized individually. Your online visibility is amplified.

Facebook Do's and Don'ts for Brands

DO:
- ✓ Spend time creating an outstanding timeline with cover photo.
- ✓ Let your brand's voice and personality shine through and be consistent.
- ✓ Reach out to people consistently, *truly* engaging with them.
- ✓ Build a loyal Facebook fanbase and thank/flatter them frequently.
- ✓ Leverage your page's posts and status updates by providing value.
- ✓ Make use of the timeline features: scheduling posts, pinning posts, featuring posts, and promoting posts.
- ✓ Work on attracting people to your site (using real value, not pushy links).

✓ Have a commenting policy in place to set page expectations.
✓ Build a community around your topic or specialty.
✓ Be proactive in intercepting and responding to feedback, positive or negative.
✓ Share relevant pictures and videos.
✓ Participate actively in conversations, but let "the people" speak!

DON'T:

☒ Be pushy.

☒ Post the same content repeatedly . . . yes, that is spam.

☒ Delete or leave idle negative feedback.

☒ Use multiple voices without notifying users with a signature or handle.

☒ Put up crude or thoughtless pictures or comments.

☒ Expect social media to "work" for you (you have to work it!).

☒ Be impatient (real relationships take time to build).

☒ Let feedback go unnoticed. Watch your stats, know where to improve, and work hard to find the right recipe for success daily!

AHA! Zen Moment

How Should You ACT on Facebook?

Attract: As cliché as it sounds, provide value to your users. Why would they like you, let alone come back to your page daily to interact with you if you don't?

Convert: You may not gain clients directly from Facebook, but you can gain consumers. Remember the value of each of those Facebook fans. If you keep them happy, they *will* bring you their business.

Transform: Facebook is a powerful platform to showcase your desire for a real relationship with your users. Your brand should profit while the consumer feels *great* about it! Have fun with it!

How to Be Proactive on Facebook

You should take the following actions *daily* on Facebook:

- Check your page for any posts (negative or positive) that need a response.
- Post or prepare content (comment on other pages, find relevant timely news to post, etc.).
- Urge your users to comment, like, or share something.
- Check any campaigns, applications, or inquiries, and tend to them.

Take the following actions *weekly*:

- Post new photos of an event, a day at the office, or something funny for users to comment on.
- Post a new video from your series if you have one or a relevant video in your industry to capture users' attention.
- Provide a link to your website (your blog, or other useful information) or other social media account (company LinkedIn page, Twitter account, etc.)—but only if for a notable reason.

Take the following actions *monthly*:

- Track how many people visited your website from Facebook and measure which articles or posted links got the most feedback. Then do more of what works!
- Strategize your content calendars, campaigns, and initiatives for the coming month, and get creative needs handled, so that you can monitor your page stress-free.

A Cautionary Note

I would be remiss if I didn't add the following warning. As you build your community on Facebook, be sure to drive it outward—to your website, your email list, and so on. Why? Because as much as you feel that you own your own brand's information and contacts on a social media site, you don't. If Facebook ever decides to ban your account (and I have seen it done, even to people who always followed the rules), you don't want to be stranded.

Facebook fan pages were created to be the official presence on Facebook for companies, nonprofits, and celebrities. Fan pages provide an incredibly rich opportunity for small and large businesses to interact with customers and fans, and find new customers and fans. You can think of fan pages as microsites . . . [They] feature Facebook applications such as Photos, Videos, Events, Reviews, and Notes, and even applications customized just for your company.

However, the major advantage of Facebook fan pages over microsites or your own company websites is that they are built on the Facebook platform—where a lot of people are spending a lot of time each day. To be precise, as of September 2009, 300 million users are on Facebook, with 1 million new users per day! Furthermore, Facebook ads allow you to "hypertarget" based on demographic information and keyword information found in profiles—not only to find out how many people in your particular target audience are on Facebook, but to reach them and draw them over to your fan page. For example, an Italian restaurant in Cleveland can choose to advertise only to men and women ages twenty-five to forty who list "Italian food" as an interest. A Dallas florist can choose to advertise only to women within a twenty-five-mile radius of Dallas who list themselves as "engaged." Once people become "fans" of your page, you can interact with them on a regular basis, just as you would interact with your friends.

No matter what your business or organization, chances are now that your customers and potential customers are using Facebook. Why not bring your business to them?

Dave Kerpen,
Chief Buzz Officer of Likeable Media (www.likeable.com)

There is a service, SocialSafe (www.SocialSafe.net), which for $2.99 will back up your profile, pictures, and a list of your friends. This is a very worthwhile investment. But even if you have this backup in place, I reiterate: use Facebook as a tool to attract, but constantly look to pull people to your site.

Twitter

The Grand Bazaar of Social Networking Sites

Why Bother with Twitter?

- It has over 500 million users as of 2012 and is continuing to grow.
- It is one of the fastest-growing social networking sites.
- 18 percent of people between 18 and 29, 14 percent of those between 30 and 49, 8 percent of those between 50 and 64, and 6 percent of those 65 and older are using Twitter (Pew Internet—June 2011).
- Teenage usage of Twitter has recently increased.
- It provides excellent online visibility.
- It's a great way to attract traffic.
- It allows for instant communication.

Twitter is like a giant, colorful bazaar.

With only the 140 characters per tweet that Twitter allows, you can attract attention and create an expert platform like never before. People use Twitter not just to connect with each other, but to share what they need, so it's *much* easier to spot people who might need your help on Twitter than it is on Facebook.

Twitter Basics

Let's start with some basic Twitter knowledge.

You get 140 characters to answer: "What are you doing?" This is the entire premise of Twitter. However, the worst thing you can do is *actually* answer that question. (I will get to that in a bit!)

Messages that people send out are called "tweets." "Tweeting" is another common phrase; it means sending a message via Twitter. Your tweets make up a timeline. When people subscribe to your timeline, or "follow" you, your tweets show up on their Twitter home page. These people are called followers. You can follow them back if you choose. Unlike Facebook, following does not have to be mutual. You can follow anyone you want, but they don't have to follow you back.

Everyone gets a Twitter name, also known as a "handle." Choose one that's short and memorable. You can thank me for this later when your followers are able to retweet your messages more easily.

You don't have to reply to all tweets. If you want to reply to someone's tweets or want to get someone's attention, type @username and then your message. For example, let's say you want to tweet me. Currently I have over 25,000 followers, and only 10 messages or so show up on my home page. If you want to get on my radar, it is most effective to tweet "at" me: @Shama.

Your home page defaults to your timeline, which shows a random assortment (chronologically) of messages tweeted by the people you are following. The following image shows my home page. When someone sends you an "@" reply, it will show up on your home page and will also be filed under the @Connect tab at the top of your home page.

You can also send direct messages to people. The 140-character limit still applies, and you can send only direct messages to people who are following you. This isn't the same as sending replies,

which can be sent to anyone using the @ sign. Direct messages are hidden from public view and shown only to the recipient. To send someone a message directly, click the icon to the right of the search bar and select "Direct Messages." This will open a window that allows you to type in the recipient's name and your message.

You don't have to use your browser to get on Twitter. You can use a desktop application. My favorite is TweetDeck (www.Tweet-Deck.com). There are also tons of mobile applications for Twitter. Just search the internet for "Twitter application + [device of your choice]" (e.g., Mac, iPad, Android, etc.).

Many Twitter users use hashtags, words that include the hash symbol (#), to keep relevant tweets organized. Hashtags were developed by the Twitter community to make it easier to search for relevant tweets. They are very popular at conferences and seminars, where many people might be twittering, because they make it easy to track what is going on at an event.

For example, during the Iranian elections, a lot of Twitter users were updating Twitter with news. They would use the hashtag #iran or #irannews, so if someone was searching for tweets on this topic, he or she could find them easily.

It's All About the Dialogue!

Although most of my friends consider me an early adopter, everything I get involved with already has at least a sprinkling of users, so I think I'm somewhere closer to the middle. Nonetheless, in the case of Twitter, I've had an account since it was a weird, unknown service with a funny name, long before Oprah and Ashton Kutcher created the race for followers and wayyy long before TV shows decided that a Twitter crawl on the bottom of the screen offered pretensions of interactivity.

Heck, in the old days, having more than 500 followers was an amazing feat, and those people who got into the four-digit follower numbers were the wizened elite, the really popular folk on the service. Now there are so many (spammy) tools to garner followers (none of whom are actually paying any attention to you) that it's common to see newbies who have thousands of followers and no clue how Twitter works.

Twitter certainly can be a one-way communication channel, a 140-character megaphone to an audience of thousands, but to do that is to miss out on what differentiates Twitter from the many other social media services available: it's interactive and lets you instantly *establish a dialogue* with your customers and community.

I know Shama gets this, but I worry that you, the reader, might not. Please, to really understand the value of Twitter and to really gain benefit from your involvement, keep in mind that you need to *give more than you expect to receive*. Don't ask, "How many followers can I blast my message to?" but instead, "How many people can I engage in a dialogue with?"

You'll be surprised just how much more enjoyable—and valuable—the experience will be.

Dave Taylor,
DaveTaylorOnline.com

Another recent and major example of global hashtag usage was #London2012 and #Olympics. The Olympics were especially popular on Twitter, as a great number of the athletes who participated had their own Twitter accounts. Brands, businesses, media outlets, and fans from countries all around the world could monitor and keep tabs on the event happenings in real time, as well as interact with other Twitter users interested in the subject.

If you will be attending a trade show or any other type of event later in the year, find out if a hashtag is being used specifically for the event and interact before, during, and after the event. By doing this, you will maximize your networking time and learn from the community where you will need to focus your time at the event.

You can see current hashtags at hashtags.org or use Twitter's search feature to see if any of the hashtags you think should exist actually do exist. Many industries have their own hashtags—e.g., #slpeeps (speech pathologists) and #eventprofs (event planning professionals)—so it is also a good way for both B2C and B2B businesses to find their audiences and start engaging.

Retweeting (RT) is reposting another person's tweet. This can have a quick viral effect when the quality of the information is good. For example, let's say you post a link from your blog. If I am following you and I like the link, I will retweet it to my followers. If you hover over a tweet you would like to pass on to your followers, you will see a "retweet" link. By clicking it you will retweet the original tweet to your followers in Twitter's default format. There are also two widely used formats for manually retweeting:

- Type "RT @username" and then copy and paste their message.
- Copy and paste their message followed by "(via @username)."

If you are using a post tool like Hootsuite, which allows you to edit a retweet (the word retweet is now in the Oxford English Dictionary), take the time to write a personal note about why you are retweeting this information. Respond and the user who you are retweeting may reply back to you with a mention. When anyone mentions you, your reach expands in the best way—it means someone is advocating for you/your Twitter name, and their followers may begin to follow you too.

When giving credit in a tweet to a source outside of Twitter, use HT. This abbreviation stands for "hat tip" or "heard through." Whether the information you are tweeting came from a blog, a conversation you saw online, or an article, it's important to give credit where it is due. Most often it is formatted as "HT: @username" or "HT: name."

Your Personal Twitter Page

Your Twitter experience starts with your Twitter page or personal profile. This is different from your profile on Facebook because it gives you less room to play with. You have to be succinct on Twitter. The following tips can help you make the most of your Twitter profile.

- Start by picking a short username. Ideally, go with your first name. Although Twitter allows you to use business names as handles, I recommend you go with your personal name. People want to be friends with people. If you are a big company looking to further your brand and provide customer service on Twitter, use your company name. If you have multiple employees using Twitter, you can create a cohandle— a handle that incorporates both the individual's name and the company's. For example, Mike-Nike and SteveCEO-Nike are cohandles.
- Use a good headshot. You don't get much space for a picture, so make sure it is large and clear and captures attention.
- The same applies to your bio. You get 160 characters for it, so be concise and direct. This isn't the place to be vague or wordy. Focus on what you do and/or who you help. Mine says: CEO of The Marketing Zen Group. Entrepreneur. Web & TV Show Host. Author. International Speaker." I could also say: "Helping businesses leverage the internet as president of The Marketing Zen Group."
- You get one web address. If you have multiple websites or multiple businesses, pick one to showcase here. I choose to

The main purpose of marketing in any institution is to tell the story behind the brand. How do you connect well with your customers in order to sell your product or service? Twitter is a great tool to use in order to show that "personality" behind a company or a brand. Use Twitter to drive people (traffic) to a blog that tells your story. Talk about your customers, clients, and your business. Twitter is a great avenue to connect with customers on a personal level, as well as on a professional level. Use it to your advantage.

Kyle Lacy,
author of Twitter Marketing for Dummies

showcase Shama.TV because it allows people to get to know me as a person better, and because I point out my business URL in my bio.

- Get and use a personalized Twitter background. This is akin to your computer's desktop background, except that on Twitter, everyone who visits your profile can see it. You can see mine at www.twitter.com/Shama. Any graphic designer can create one for you. We create them on occasion for our clients as well. Why? It's a great marketing tool, and it will set you apart! You don't get to say a lot using your 160-character bio, but you can make a great impression using your Twitter background. Make sure it includes your name, a way to reach you (email, phone, or both), your major websites, and a brief bio. Keep it clutter free, use your brand colors, and again, be succinct!

- Be sure to upload your photos (up to 3 MB) using Twitter Galleries (which began rolling out to all users in August 2011) to populate your four "Recent Images" in the space below your Twitter profile and under "Lists." You'll notice it creates a pic.twitter link for the tweet. If you attach a hashtag to your pictures, they will show up in Twitter's video and photo search. Note: At least for the moment, Twitter galleries are limited to the 100 most recent images associated with a Twitter account.

Who to Follow

On Twitter, you can choose to follow everyone you find and amass diverse tweets or you can choose to follow a specific few from whom you derive value. I follow a variety of people, and it makes for a very robust Twitter experience. If you are interested in someone's tweets, follow him or her. Don't worry about whether he or she follows you back. You will attract your own group of followers.

Here are a few tips to get started:

- Upload your contact list, and see who is already on Twitter. You may be surprised. To do this, click on the #Discover tab, and select "Search Contacts" next to the email provider that you use.
- Look for more people you know. Twitter has a search tool that allows you to search for people using keywords and names.
- Feel free to follow me (@Shama). I will follow back. (My open-door policy applies on Twitter as well!)
- If you belong to another social media site, announce that you are now on Twitter. Be sure to give your username. Status updates on Facebook and LinkedIn are a great way to make announcements like this.

Marketing via Twitter represents a very unique and compelling channel for marketers. Its ease of use, transactional speed, pure text format, and ability to reach a large audience in 140 characters offers simplicity and yet complexity. For big brands, the ability to connect directly with consumers offers a free fall of both good and bad feedback, and many are using Twitter as a customer service channel. Furthermore, for transactional products, a very compelling promotion can get unbelievable reach and offer a potential viral impact. For individuals, social media influence is driven by content and relationships. Many have built strong personal brands with Twitter by sharing and creating content and engaging individuals and companies.

Mike D. Merrill,
MikeMerrill.com

- Once you have at least five followers, look at who they follow. If they seem interesting, follow them.
- Use Twellow.com, WeFollow.com, and FollowerWonk.com, directories of people on Twitter organized by industry and interest. You can look for people to follow and list yourself as well. For example, if you are a PR pro, you'd want to look for reporters so that if they need a source for a story, you are there. Follow people within niches: industry, city, occupation, and so on. It is a great way to meet locals.
- Check to see if your favorite bloggers, actors, or media personalities are on Twitter. Chances are they are. Follow them. Often they are easier to get in touch with via Twitter because it only takes them a few characters to respond.
- See who the people you follow recommend. I often recommend good people to follow. There is a current trend on Twitter called Follow Friday. Twitterers recommend who they follow to their followers followed by the #followfriday or #ff hashtag on Fridays. (You follow?)

How to Make the Most of Twitter

Think of Twitter as a global human search engine. It is completely what you make of it.

Let me give you an example. I was scheduled to speak to a group of CEOs at an organization called Vistage that I had never spoken to before. The group's host had forewarned me that this could be a tough crowd because they often really grilled their speakers. Hearing this, I did a quick search on Twitter for "Vistage Speakers" and found five. Using the @ sign, I asked them if they had any recommendations. Within two minutes, I had a variety of responses like "use statistics and case studies" and "Best of luck! Let us know how it goes." Folks I had never met before—one in China—were wishing me well.

This same experience has repeated itself in various areas. When I first got my dog, Snoopy, I had no idea what it was like to raise a puppy. I'd frequently turn to my Twitter followers and ask, "Do puppies eat peanuts?" or, "My puppy sleeps a lot! Is that normal?" I always get excellent answers.

Tom Morris, writer and philosopher, wrote an insightful article called "Twisdom: Twitter Wisdom" for the *Huffington Post* (www.HuffingtonPost.com, September 9, 2009). Morris writes:

> Twitter is not mainly about telling the world, or your forty-seven followers, what you had for lunch. And it's not just about Ashton and Oprah, or who can attract the most followers the quickest. It's about building a new form of community. It's about learning. It's about support, inspiration, and daily motivation. And it's also about fun. But the most important aspect of Twitter may be that, if you do things right, you begin to surround yourself with an incredible group of people eager to share their best questions and insights about life. They're all looking for new wisdom and hope. Twisdom is the result.
>
> There's collaborative thinking on Twitter at a level and in a form I've never seen before. Almost every day, and often many times a day, a topic comes up that causes me, as a philosopher and simply a curious individual, to ponder a bit, and then share the results of that pondering in the 140 character increments, or "tweets" that Twitter allows. One comment will spark another, and before long, people of different ages and walks of life from around the world are engaged with me and each other in an extended conversation of brief bursts that add up to new realizations for everyone involved.

Multiple Twitter Accounts

Can you have multiple Twitter accounts? Yes. Should you have multiple accounts? It depends. Some people have an account for business twittering and another for personal twittering. I think this is a difficult balance to maintain because it is tough enough to get traction going for one Twitter account. However, it can be done. Dave Taylor (www.AskDaveTaylor.com)

does a great job with his business account (www.twitter.com/FilmBuzz) and maintains a personal account as well. I have seen others successfully maintain business accounts, offering coupons, monetary deals, and so on. There are also service-oriented accounts that tweet current deals or respond to customer service issues. There are news services that tweet only headlines. You can choose what type of an account you want. Be careful, though: it needs to be something that people value or enjoy. Dave's business account is successful at least partially because film trivia and reviews are something that people enjoy more often than not.

Following and Un-following

We've discussed who you should follow, but can you un-follow someone who isn't providing value? Absolutely. If someone you follow doesn't add value to your life, feel free to stop following him or her. This is not an etiquette issue.

How do you get people to follow you? Try the following.

- Don't answer Twitter's question ("What are you doing?") literally. No one really cares about the fact that you just brushed your teeth or have to go pick up the kids from school, unless you can make it valuable. Avoid saying, "Going to pick up kids." Instead, say, "Picking up kids from school. I-35 and Beltline are jammed. Find another route." That's helpful!
- Leave out mundane details *unless* they add value. Avoid things like, "Loving this veggie burger." Use, "Loving this veggie burger at the new San Francisco joint on 45th and Lemon @VeggieTimeSF."
- Share valuable content. If you find a great site or useful tidbit, share. It's also okay to share content that you wrote yourself, as long as it's useful. My company gets 20 percent of our website traffic from Twitter using this method. Note: If you are sharing feedback on a place you've just visited, the latest article you've read, or someone's video link, see if

you can find the creator's Twitter name and be sure to mention them in your tweet. This makes it much more likely that they will see your tweet and gives you a greater chance of being retweeted (further expanding your reach to a new group of followers).

- Ask genuine questions and welcome feedback. While writing this book, I often turned to my Twitter followers and asked what they would like to see addressed. Thoughtful questions can also lead to engaging discussions that can help you better understand others' perspectives and obtain feedback. This is key to building relationships.

- Put a button on your blog or website that invites people to follow you. One of the buttons we are most thankful for right now is Twitter's very own Follow button, a small widget that can be easily integrated onto a website. Your site's visitors can quickly click the small "Follow" button without leaving your site, and you've gained a follower on Twitter. Another thing you can do to promote your Twitter presence is designate a plot of your website real estate to a Twitter feed. This is a widget that can greatly liven up your site and give your visitors some real-time updates straight from your mouth...uh, keyboard. The Twitter button can be found at https://dev.twitter.com/docs/follow-button.

- Make it a point to follow at least two new interesting people per day and send them a quick note commenting on how much value you've found reading their tweets. They may follow you back!

- Host a contest or giveaway. Many high-profile bloggers have done this. They ask people to follow them and retweet their contest message to enter the contest, so their name is spread quickly. This works if (1) you already have a good following (at least a few hundred), and (2) the giveaway is solid. You can also partner with industry-related bloggers or influencers who have Twitter accounts and have them host the contest for you. (You provide the prize, of course!)

- Don't ask people to help you get more followers to reach a certain number. It looks awful. It is okay to ask *if* you have a goal that isn't about your follower number. Avoid saying, "Please help me get to 500 followers. I am so close. Thanks." Instead, try, "I'd love to meet more people in the Detroit area. Can you recommend any?"
- When tweeting links, shorten them using a URL-shortening service. This way, you can fit more characters into a single tweet. Also, many URL-shortening services, like goog.gl, ow.ly, and bit.ly, allow you to track how many clicks a link receives. This is a great way to figure out what attracts folks to your website—and then do more of it!

Do the numbers matter? Yes. I wish I could say that they don't, but the number of people who follow you does matter. Why? The more people who follow you, the greater the reach you have. Today, when I ask a question or need feedback on an idea, I get 10 to 20 replies very quickly—and that's with 22,000 followers. So, yes, numbers matter.

Does this mean that you should obsess over the number of people following you? No. It's still better to focus on a smaller pool of people with whom you have connected rather than thousands with whom you haven't. You want to manage quality carefully as you increase quantity. As more and more people follow you, you can find tools that will help you categorize and organize the tweets. If you use TweetDeck, for example, you can organize your followers into categories. I have mine set up into two rows. The first contains all my followers, and the second is a list of colleagues and personal friends.

A Word on Auto-Following and Automated Direct Messaging

There are many applications out there that will allow you to auto-follow, meaning automatically following back those who follow you. There are also applications that let you do automated direct messaging, in which you send a canned direct message to all your followers. I don't recommend either technique.

When Twitter was new, automatically following people was a good way to give kudos (if you follow me, I will follow you back) and to grow your network. However, because Twitter has grown so rapidly, it has attracted its share of spammers. Unlike Facebook, which monitors and suspends accounts for even remotely suspicious activity, Twitter takes a more laissez-faire approach in governing. Spammers are notorious for following people who auto-follow and then un-following them. This skews their count so it looks like 10,000 people are following them and they are only following a handful. Can you think of any reason why 10,000 people would follow a spammer? Of course not. This is the whole point of their trick. They make it seem like they are legitimate by taking advantage of those who auto-follow.

Automated direct messaging is also a huge Twitter don't. There was a time when I believed automated messages could work when used properly, but because of Twitter's growth and users' misuse of the function by spammers, I recommend against it.

Using Twitter to Attract, Convert, and Transform

Twitter is one of those rare social networking sites where you can do all three! You can attract people to your website, convert followers into consumers and customers, and transform your past successes by sharing stories and case studies.

Posting links is a great way to attract people to your website. I once wrote a post called "10 Things to Do Immediately After a Networking Event" that included a link to our company blog. It led to 1,125 visits to our company blog when I tweeted it (and others retweeted it). That one article with a link attracted over a thousand people! Of that thousand, many chose to subscribe to the blog, becoming permanent consumers. Some will go on to convert into clients.

There are also times when we find people tweeting to search for something—such as web design, SEO, or social media help—in lieu of asking a friend or using a search engine. When we find such folks, we offer—without being pushy—to help them. It's even better when someone who is following us tells them, "Hey,

The Marketing Zen Group does that kind of work well. Connect with @Shama." Often that turns them into an instant client for us!

Then, when we do the work, we share our results. For example, I might say, "Just launched a new website for Sal's Pizza! Check it out here: www.sals-pizza.com. That was a great project!" Or, we might share a case study or a story. This is difficult to do in 140 characters, but it can be accomplished with some practice. For example: "Client needed to reach a very targeted audience. Set up a Facebook page and targeted group XYZ. Got 800 clicks and a 20% increase in sales."

Getting Started on Twitter: The Power of Influencers

This content was originally shared as a post on The Marketing Zen Group blog, but we've decided to add it into the book because it details a strategy that can truly make or break your Twitter launch, and get you moving toward Twitter stardom. Now that we've covered how to set up a profile, it's time to make Twitter work for you.

The day you decide to get your blog/company/brand/self on Twitter is the same day you should commit to reaching out to at least ten people/companies/organizations multiple times in the coming weeks; let's call these people your "influencers."

Please note, when I say influencers I am referring to Twitter users who excel in the following:

- Valuable Content (their content is engaging, relevant, useful/unique)
- Appropriate Frequency (they tweet daily, with a good number of posts/day)
- High Quality Interaction (they are not spammers or RT-addicts)

If the users you discover have these three items nailed down, it is highly probable that they have been listed and followed by many others. It is important that you find a handful of influencers to interact with rather than just start sending out tweets to every other person you come across, because the right influencers are the people that can help you extend your reach, heighten your visibility, and ultimately gain Twitter followers for your blog/business/organization/self.

Your First Task: Write a List of Keywords

Write a list of keywords (to search for on Twitter), including industry occupations and common glossary terms, that would help direct you to:

- Twitter users in your industry (businesses/organizations/associations)
- Twitter users who write about your industry (media/industry journals and publications)
- Twitter users who are your competitors

Writing your list digitally is best so that you can copy/paste keywords into Twitter's search field when you're ready to discover your influencers.

Your Second Task: The Big Twitter Search-Off

- Search your top keywords, popular competitors, and industry associations.
- See who:
  a) they are following
  b) is mentioning them
  c) is following them
  d) is listing them
  e) is RT-ing them
  ...all in that order.
- Start clicking on the Twitter usernames you see, and look through their lists to find new and interesting people you'd like to follow.
- If you find a potential influencer, add them to your potential influencers list for any future marketing or PR efforts.

(See "Searching Twitter to Join Relevant Conversations" for more search tips.)

Your Third Task: Investigate

After you've compiled a list of Twitter users-of-interest, ask your-self the following questions:

- Is their content valuable to your audiences? (Is it engaging, relevant, useful/unique?)
- Was their last post yesterday? Are they tweeting three to eight posts throughout the day, every/almost every day, and including a mix of original content, RTs, and Mentions?
- Are their interactions (RTs and Mentions) relevant to your business/industry/audiences?

Extra Credit Task: Record the list of Twitter users you find, giving them grades. Here is a basic "Twitter Influencer Grade Report" format:

- Twitter Handle | Type of Product/Service/Business | Follow-ers: # | Listed: #
- Twitter Profile Bio:
- URL:
- Tweet:
- Frequency:
- Level: Low – Med – High
- Score: 1 or 2
  1: Great content you would share with your audience; looks like they would be interested in sharing your content; influencer potential.
  2: Too many personal tweets and RTs and not enough original/valuable/relevant information or interaction with other users.

Your Fourth Task: Pick Your Top Ten Influencers and Go!

Analyze the grade report you developed during task 3. This report is something you can quickly scan and use to determine the first ten people you will try to develop a relationship with (through sharing valuable content, mutual RTing, and mentioning). Look at how you've ranked them and choose ten to start out with based on the areas most important to you. Note: It may be hard to keep up with more than ten when you're just getting started or if you are the lone social media resource for your company.

Once you have your ten, make your presence known and begin building those relationships!

- Make sure that your feed is fairly developed when you start reaching out to your influencers; i.e., do not have three tweets on your profile with promotional messaging and zero original tweets. Start out with a welcome tweet with a quick blurb of the purpose of your Twitter profile. Then RT a few relevant articles and craft a few posts related to your activity as a blogger/company/interest (something your potential followers will connect with and find value in).
- RT their original content. Mention them and give your opinion and/or ask questions about their statements in a piece of content they've produced. They will likely reply to you by mentioning your name (if your note sounds genuine and is not attacking them). If your tweet is as valuable/innovative/smart/relevant to the influencer's audience as it should be, the influencer's audience may look into following you too.
- Thank them for sharing a valuable tip. Write a custom message for your audience on why it is a good link and mention the influencer at the end of it, so they are alerted of your "review." They will likely RT your tweet because of its positive testimony.

It is always important—no matter where you are sharing/posting/tweeting content—to ask yourself, how would I respond to this messaging? If you critique your message with this question in mind and find yourself feeling negatively about it, it is time to try again. Remember, you are projecting information to humans who can tell trash from treasure within an instant.

Searching Twitter to Join Relevant Conversations

Knowing how to search on Twitter is crucial because that is how you know which conversations to join! Practicing savvy searching skills on Twitter is like practicing good listening skills in a face-to-face conversation. If you don't search, you won't know who is looking for you—and, perhaps more importantly, who might have a complaint or concern. Complaints and concerns are best addressed publicly so others can see that you are a company that cares and is tuned in. Many big companies such as Comcast, Dell, and JetBlue use Twitter to offer customer service. They search for mentions of their name and engage those users in a useful conversation.

You can search Twitter conversations directly from your Twitter home page. You can also set up keyword alerts (similar to Google alerts) using a service like TweetBeep. What should you search for? Your company name, your personal name, and any industry-related terms. Also, be sure to search for phrases related to the service or product you offer. For example, if you are a web designer, you should search for "need website." This is one of the beautiful things about Twitter. People *often* search for what they need in a very public manner. It is not uncommon to see people asking for referrals and recommendations. *And* it is okay to offer up your product or company in a nonintrusive manner. Recently, I was searching for some project-management software, and I asked for recommendations. Shortly afterward, two owners of project-management software companies asked whether I had seen their site and if I would like a demo. This is a great example of selling made simple. Best of all, because I was looking for this information, I was grateful to hear from them.

Here are three stories on how I have leveraged Twitter to further my own business:

1. **Snagged a speaking engagement:** I follow the founder of a very prestigious blogging conference. I had just submitted my speaking proposal through his website when I sent him a public message giving him a heads-up on the proposed topic. No sooner had I sent out that tweet than a well-known blogger retweeted the message and added something along the lines of "you would be missing out if she didn't present." Almost immediately, I got a direct message from the founder saying he liked the topic and that I was in. It all happened within seconds! Don't underestimate the power of Twitter. Since then, people have often noticed my speaking topics when I tweet and asked me to speak at their events.

2. **Found direct clients:** We get at least two leads a week from Twitter. Someone inevitably sees a tweet about a website we just finished, or a ranking we achieved for a client, and

wants to know what we can do for him or her. That is social media at its best, because you are attracting new clients by transforming your old successes into stories—or, in this case, tweets!

3. **Established expertise**: We once had a client who hired us solely by looking at my tweets. He said they were proof that we knew online marketing; our tips on Twitter convinced him. Establishing my expertise has led to multiple speaking opportunities, more clients, and articles in various publications. It has also led to some great joint venture relationships. Colleagues who do complementary work will often see what we do and refer their clients to us. It is a win-win situation for all.

Some Useful Tools for Twitter Search

Get help from Twitter:
- Twitter's Guide to Search: bit.ly/SearchTW
- Twitter's Advanced Search: twitter.com/#!/search-advanced

Find relevant Twitter users faster:
- WeFollow.com
- Twellow.com
- FollowerWonk.com

Find relevant Twitter lists (following uber-relevant users) faster:
- Listorious.com

Find local Twitter users with:
- TwitterLocal.net
- Twellow.com/twellowhood
- LocalTweeps.com

Twitter Applications

Because Twitter continues to grow at such a fast pace, applications to bolster it are being created on a daily basis. Here are few of my favorites:

- Timely.is (timely.is): Timely automatically schedules your tweets during the time they will have the most impact on your specific audiences and can be used for multiple accounts. We're not completely sure how exact the system behind Timely is, but we've found it to be quite interesting, successful, and simple to use.
- Gremln (www.gremln.com): Gremln allows you to schedule your tweets, create groups, manage multiple users, and monitor your brand.
- TweetDeck (www.TweetDeck.com): TweetDeck allows you to manage Twitter on your desktop. It shows you the tweets of people you're following, replies, and direct messages in three clean columns. No clicking back and forth necessary!
- SocialOomph (www.SocialOomph.com): SocialOomph allows you to release tweets in the future. Going on a vacation but found some good content to share? You can use this application to write tweets ahead of time to post automatically while you're gone.
- SocialToo (www.SocialToo.com): Similar to SocialOomph, SocialToo also allows you to filter tweets to avoid spammers and sets up surveys that your Twitter followers can take—a great way to get feedback.
- HootSuite (HootSuite.com): HootSuite allows you to track multiple accounts and supports multiple users. It also lets you track statistics such as how many people clicked on your last link.
- TwitPic (www.TwitPic.com): TwitPic allows you to share pictures on Twitter. It's very easy to use! However, due to Twitter's latest image integration project, Galleries, TwitPic's future is a little uncertain.
- TweetBeep (TweetBeep.com): TweetBeep allows you to set up email alerts for keywords that you want to follow on Twitter.
- Twitterfeed (Twitterfeed.com): Twitterfeed is a service that feeds your blog to Twitter. Use it in moderation! You don't want your Twitter stream to be full of your own posts.

You can see a continually updated list of newly created Twitter applications at www.birdsallsocialmedia.com/2009/04/04/birdsall%E2%80%99s-massive-twitter-sites-tools-directory.

Twitter on Your Phone?

There are a number of applications that allow you to tweet using your phone, as well. Here are a few:

- Twitterific (Twitterrific.com): Twitterific is a tried-and-true application for the iPhone.
- ÜberTwitter (www.UberTwitter.com): ÜberTwitter is a good tool for using Twitter on your BlackBerry.
- Twitter Mobile (m.twitter.com): Twitter Mobile is Twitter's own mobile site.
- TweetDeck: TweetDeck for mobile is basically as good as the desktop version.

Twitter Do's and Don'ts

DO:

- ✓ Use your tweets strategically. Know what you are trying to accomplish with your tweet.
- ✓ Follow people you admire, even if they don't follow you back.
- ✓ Be on the lookout for valuable content to share with your followers.
- ✓ Treat your followers with respect. There are lots of viewpoints on Twitter, and without nonverbal cues, it's easy to offend people. Use sarcasm with care.
- ✓ Respond to direct messages and @ replies.
- ✓ Create a community of colleagues.
- ✓ Ask genuine questions—you'll get good answers!
- ✓ Retweet when someone shares something valuable.
- ✓ Share relevant pictures and videos.
- ✓ Work on attracting people to your site (using real value, not pushy links).
- ✓ Share mini–case studies about your successes.

✓ Learn to tell stories in 140 characters.
✓ Track how many people click on your tweeted links, RT your content, and follow people who mention and RT you.

DON'T:

☒ Try to force anyone to follow you. I have seen people get angry because someone won't follow them back. You can only decide who to follow—not who follows you.

☒ Ask someone why they un-followed you. Respect their decision.

☒ Mass-follow people. (Really *look* at who you want to follow. This is your chance to create your own human search engine.)

☒ Post links only to *your* website. (No one likes someone who constantly self-promotes.)

☒ Twitter when sleepy or inebriated.

☒ Ask followers to help you reach a certain number of followers.

☒ Promote something you haven't tried yourself, just to make a few bucks.

☒ Tweet something you wouldn't want someone to find. (Tweets are indexed by Google and can come up in people's search results.)

AHA! Zen Moment

How should you ACT on Twitter?

Attract: Use a custom-designed Twitter background to showcase your website address. Post links to helpful content on your website.

Convert: Use your tweets strategically. The beauty of Twitter is that you can gain instant consumers and clients. Invite people to comment on your blog and share your content. Let them know if you are having a sale or have an opening for a client. Just be careful not to go overboard.

Transform: Tell quick stories, and share case studies in a nutshell. Proud of a project you just completed? Share it! Did a client tell you they love you? Share it! Toot your own horn, but do it gracefully and genuinely. People are smart and can usually sense when you aren't being genuine. 🧘

How to Be Proactive on Twitter
The following tips will help you use Twitter proactively.

- **Get instant market feedback.** When I asked my followers on Twitter which they would prefer—an ebook or a whole course on social media marketing—I immediately got answers and rationales. Twitter is a *great* way to test out your ideas before taking them any further. You do need to have a few hundred followers for this to be a successful test.
- **Show your followers respect.** There are companies out there who will pay you to tweet ads in the form of links. The bigger your follower base, the more you get paid. This is an awful way to monetize on Twitter. I have seen the backlash firsthand when I tested a service called Magpie. It doesn't matter if you actually have used the products you are advertising; people see it as an intrusion. Don't advertise outside products using Twitter.
- **Let people sample your style and work.** If blogs and websites are novels, tweets are short stories. Twitter is a great way to allow people to taste a sample of your work. Tweet tips related to your industry, and let your personality shine through. If you are witty, be witty. If you are known for your warm nature, show that to the world!
- **Generate quality traffic.** You can generate some quality traffic from Twitter because followers have already sampled your work or style. They may even feel like they already know you! The best traffic is generated when you share a content link from your website and people retweet it.

- **Build trust.** Social media is very much about transparency. The lines between personal and professional are blurred. Twitter is your chance to build trust with influencers and future clients and customers just by being yourself! We trust people with whom we come into contact more than we trust strangers.
- **Generate content.** Twitter is the #1 spot to find guest bloggers and interviewees. Have a blog? A podcast? Want to interview someone? Twitter is a great way to reach out to him or her!
- **Generate ideas.** If you just "listen in" on Twitter, you can see immediately that it is a marketplace buzzing with ideas. People are asking questions (that you can potentially provide answers to) and sharing thoughts. There are many movers and shakers on Twitter!
- **Get online PR.** As noted previously, bloggers hang out on Twitter a lot. And you know what bloggers have? Communities of followers. Twitter is a great way to make friends with bloggers and reporters. Be genuine. They need stories as much as you need the press.
- **Find people to hire.** There are some very talented folks on Twitter. Whenever we are hiring, we look there first by sending out a tweet to let our followers know we are hiring, and by searching specific phrases such as "web developer + Dallas." We have hired two interns we found on Twitter.
- **Manage your reputation.** Every day I see at least three people or companies being talked about that are not on Twitter and probably don't have a clue as to what is being said about them. Don't be like them. Twitter is a great way to see what people have to say about your service and product. You can also use Twitter as a customer service tool, answering questions and taking queries live. Already give great customer service? Perfect! Use Twitter to make it transparent.
- **Send out your newsletter.** Many newsletter services these days will send out a link to your newsletter through your

Twitter account when they send out your newsletter via email. iContact (www.icontact.com), AWeber (www.AWeber.com), MailChimp (www.MailChimp.com), Constant Contact (www.constantcontact.com), and Blue Sky Factory (www.BlueSkyFactory.com) all have this feature.

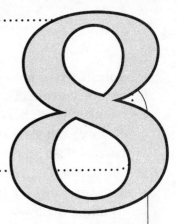

> "LinkedIn is a business-oriented social networking site founded in December 2002 and mainly used for professional networking."
>
> Wikipedia

LinkedIn
The Place Where Professionals Go

Why Bother with LinkedIn?

- It has 120 million users from over 200 countries.
- It's a network geared toward professionals looking to network—the members are there to talk shop!
- It is excellent for online visibility.
- It's a great way to showcase expertise.
- It serves as the ultimate online Rolodex.

LinkedIn is like a buttoned-down office-networking event. If Facebook is happy hour, LinkedIn is all business, in a suit and tie. It's especially useful to those in the business-to-business (B2B) sphere because it allows you to connect to specific decision-makers better than any other.

LinkedIn Basics

LinkedIn is a great way to connect with former bosses, colleagues, and clients. Chances are they are there!

LinkedIn offers both free and paid accounts. A paid account allows you to send InMails (email messages within LinkedIn) to those who are accepting them. This is a good way to reach people who may not currently be in your network. A paid account is not necessary, however, to make the most of LinkedIn.

LinkedIn allows you to give and receive professional recommendations, and you can choose to feature these on your profile. This is an excellent feature to showcase your aptitude and talent. Much of LinkedIn is about creating an interactive résumé for yourself.

Everything you need to know about LinkedIn can be divided into five segments: your profile, managing contacts, LinkedIn answers, LinkedIn groups, and LinkedIn events.

LinkedIn is really your résumé on steroids. The site has a number of advanced applications that allow you to promote your products, services, events, businesses, and brand, and drive targeted traffic to your websites. It also ranks extremely high in Google's search engine, which gives you another platform to promote your name when someone searches for you.

If you want to bring your business or brand to the next level, then it is critical to take action and start optimizing LinkedIn to achieve your goals.

Lewis Howes,
coauthor of LinkedWorking

Your LinkedIn Profile

Think of your LinkedIn profile as an interactive online résumé. Your colleagues, prospects, and vendors can all see your professional life in a nutshell. Here is a screenshot of the first part of my profile:

Use the following tips to create the best LinkedIn profile for yourself.

• Use a good headshot, ideally one that frames your full face and shows you smiling! (You can use the same one across all social media sites.)

- When you receive recommendations from colleagues and clients, showcase them on your profile. When someone posts a recommendation, you will get a message asking you to accept.
- Your summary is key. Write it to be read. Use adjectives, and make it pack a punch. It's okay if you have to rewrite it a few times. It can (and should) be a work in progress. Here is a screenshot of my current summary:

Summary

Web and TV show host. Bestselling author. International speaker. Award winning CEO of The Marketing Zen Group – a global online marketing and PR firm. Shama is the face of today's digital world, and represents the best her generation has to offer. She has aptly been dubbed the "master millennial of the universe" and "an online marketing shaman" by Fast Company.com.

Shama holds a Masters degree in Organizational Communication from the University of Texas at Austin, and prides herself in being a constant learner. Through her web marketing company, Shama works with businesses and organizations around the world. In 2009, Business Week honored Shama as one of the Top 25 under 25 entrepreneurs in North America. In 2010, Shama won the prestigious Technology Titan Emerging Company CEO award. In 2011, Entrepreneur Magazine featured her as one of four Super Sonic Youth, dubbing her a "Zen Master of Marketing."

When not working directly with her clients or shooting her shows for the media, Shama travels the world speaking on business, entrepreneurship, and technology. The 2nd edition of her best-selling book, The Zen of Social Media Marketing, is due out in the spring of 2012.

Specialties

Digital Marketing, Online Marketing, Social Media Marketing, Outsource Marketing, Web Design and Development, Blog Design and Development, Search Engine Optimization, Professional Speaker, Facebook Marketing, Entrepreneurship, Digital Trends, Technology

---

- In your summary, use keywords that make it easy for other people to search for you. Include industry terms as well as layman's terms. For example, for the longest time, the airline industry thought everyone was searching for "low airfare," only to discover that most were looking for "cheap tickets."
- Remember to check your spelling. This is a professional networking site, and the rules (though unwritten) are a bit more stringent. Whereas someone may forgive a spelling slipup on Twitter or Facebook, on LinkedIn misspelling a word is comparable to making a spelling error on your résumé.

• The "specialties" area directly beneath your summary allows you to "tag" yourself appropriately. Think about how others may categorize you or search for you. What keywords would you want someone to use to find you? Also, what specifically do you specialize in? You will notice that in my specialties section I include "online marketing" (which is very broad so people can find me under that category) and also "Facebook marketing" (which is a specialty).

• LinkedIn allows you to make your profile public. If you are planning to use LinkedIn as a marketing tool, by all means make it public. This allows search engines to find you as well, making keyword usage even more important.

Managing Contacts

Who should you connect with on LinkedIn?

- Past and current bosses: It's especially important to add those with whom you have a good relationship; they are great folks to get recommendations from.
- Your clients and customers: If you have a huge list of customers, only add those with whom you have connected personally via email or phone. In other words, add only those who would recognize your name!
- Industry contacts such as vendors, distributors, and resellers: Essentially, add all business contacts.
- Bloggers who cover your industry or might cover your product: Not all bloggers will be open to connecting on LinkedIn, but some will.

LinkedIn Answers

LinkedIn's "answers" section is an area where you can ask and answer questions. This is a great way to showcase your expertise. Sometimes companies that use this feature are also looking for referrals. If your company is a fit or what they're looking for, you can definitely approach them. But above all, the LinkedIn answers feature is perfect for two things:

1. **Market research:** I once asked what people wished to learn more about within the field of online marketing. Social media marketing was on top of the list! You can also answer questions that others post. The following is a screenshot that shows some questions asked under the internet marketing category. I can see that someone is curious to know if it is okay to use Twitter to generate leads. By clicking on this question, I can go to a page that shows me the full

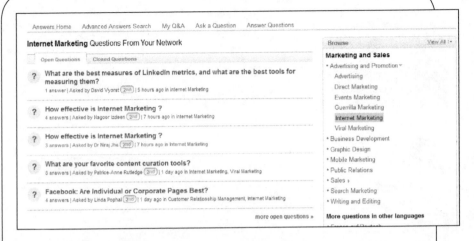

question and gives me the option to answer it. Or I can answer on my blog and post the reply link to the question. I can then share that same post across my social networks.

2. **Showcasing expertise**: When a LinkedIn member asks a question, he or she also gets to choose the best answer. LinkedIn uses a rating system to award points to the person whose answer is chosen. This can be showcased on your profile with a badge that says, for example, "Public Relations (5 best answers)." This is a nice boost in credibility when someone is looking at your profile for the first time.

LinkedIn Groups

LinkedIn groups are similar to Facebook groups. They're a great way to find people with similar interests. Once you have joined a group, it will appear on your left-side navigation bar under "Groups." Here are some ways LinkedIn groups can be useful:

- **They let you send InMail to members without having to upgrade.** This feature itself makes LinkedIn groups useful. If you try to message someone who isn't connected to you, LinkedIn will ask you to upgrade. Join a group that that person is a member of, and you can send him or her a message without upgrading. Again, this works best if you have

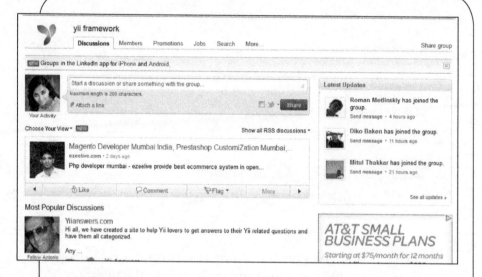

a genuine interest in the group and aren't using this feature as a spam mechanism.

- **They're a great way to communicate with your group or organization online.** Look under the "Discussions" tab on your group page to view current discussions or start your own.
- **Those searching for you can find you more easily.** If someone is searching for a speaker, he or she is likely to find you more easily if you are already part of a LinkedIn speaker's group.

To find groups to join, look through LinkedIn's group directory at www.linkedin.com/groupsDirectory. (You can also find a link to this directory under "Groups" in the left navigation bar of your profile page.) In certain groups, your membership may have to be reviewed by a group manager before you are accepted. For instance, college- or company-related groups may require an email address associated with the college or company. If you have questions about a group, you can send a message to the owner listed on the group information page.

LinkedIn Events

You can gain access to the LinkedIn Events feature by logging in, clicking "More" from the home page navigation, and scrolling down to Events. The Event feature lets you know about upcoming conferences and industry events. It pulls events from sites such as www.EventBrite.com and makes recommendations for

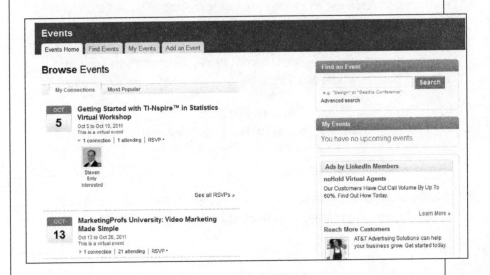

you based on your industry and the contents of your profile. It also allows you to search for events. It is a great way to see what hot events are occurring in your industry. You can also see which of your connections on LinkedIn will be attending. It isn't LinkedIn's most exciting feature, but it is one more way you can connect with others.

LinkedIn Do's and Don'ts

For the ultimate do's and don'ts on LinkedIn, I reached out to Jason Alba (CEO of JibberJobber and author of *I'm on LinkedIn— Now What???*), Mike O'Neil (CEO of Integrated Alliances), and Viveka von Rosen (Always Extraordinary). I asked all three LinkedIn experts to provide me with unique do's and don'ts that

Be the One with the Answers

Answering questions on LinkedIn is a proven strategy for positioning you or your business as the go-to resource in your niche. Like most marketing tactics, the more strategic and personalized your answer is, the better your results.

So, how does your response to a question get ranked as a best answer? The person who asks the question selects one best and several good answers for each question. Receiving a LinkedIn best answer ranking means you show up in the results and adds to your credibility.

When your answer is selected as the best, thank the person who asked the question. To give your answers life beyond LinkedIn, repurpose your comments as a blog post, an article, or a feature in your organization's communications.

Barbara Rozgonyi,
author of The Top 10 Ways to Quickly Become
a Subject Matter Expert Using LinkedIn

are often overlooked. The first five tips in each list were provided by Jason; the rest were provided by Mike and Viveka.

DO:
- ✓ **Flesh out your profile.** Too many profiles are sparse, with little information. Not only does this decrease your chances of being found when someone is searching for talent, but when someone does find your profile, he or she doesn't have much to go on.
- ✓ **Participate in LinkedIn Answers.** This might be the best way to communicate with your contacts, which is critical in nurturing relationships. Use the Answers feature to stimulate conversation and gather information.
- ✓ **Join groups.** When you join groups, you have extra privileges with group members that you would only have if you were first-degree contacts. This is also a great way to find people who share like interests without having to find them in search results.

✓ **Use the advanced search.** This is a very powerful part of LinkedIn and can help you find contacts you should get in touch with or add to your network. Go beyond the basic search and explore the power of the advanced search.

✓ **Export your contacts.** On the Contacts page, toward the bottom, there is an "Export Connections" link. I recommend you do so to create a backup, and also take it a step further: import them into a CRM (customer relationship management) tool. That way you can manage the relationships with more detail without being subject to LinkedIn's restrictions.

✓ **Treat your LinkedIn profile like a website.** Make sure it is well-formatted, clean, and, most importantly, of interest to others. Ask friends to read it, and ask them to be very critical in their assessments. This should not be an "attaboy" moment.

✓ **Populate your LinkedIn profile with keywords.** The keywords should reflect your background, your industry, and the industries of your *clients* to make it easier for potential clients to find you. Be sure to include the variants of the words (teach, teacher, taught, teaching), the synonyms of those words (speaker, educator), and the variants of *those* words (speaking, education).

✓ **Make your page visually interesting.** Look into using special symbols (➔ ◊ ■ ↔ ♦) to break up your text and add emphasis to key elements.

DON'T:

☒ **Spam.** Don't come to LinkedIn hoping to hawk your wares. This is a place to network, and business happens here, but people want to focus on relationships, not listen to your next cool pitch. Make sure you are authentic and care about them before you start talking too much about your company or product.

☒ **Forget who might see your profile.** Getting too casual or too serious, or not being compelling enough, might cost you in business or opportunities. Have your profile ready for your target audience, and when they find it, you'll have the credibility you need.

☒ **Misunderstand the concept of connections.** Will you connect with everyone? What about your competition? Or will you connect with only people you have met in person? Everyone has a different connection strategy appropriate to him or her. You need to figure out your own connection strategy.

☒ **Send canned invitations.** When you invite someone, go into the invitation message and customize it. Let him or her know who you are and why you want to connect.

☒ **Preach.** I get invitations on LinkedIn telling me all the virtues of LinkedIn. When I see these invitations, I know the senders have not read my profile, and I assume they are just adding me to increase their numbers (as opposed to wanting to develop a relationship with me).

☒ **Use anything in your name field that doesn't belong as part of your name.** For example, don't use "Paul A. (Pablo_paul@yahoo.com), PABLO A." when you can use "Pablo Paul," or LinkedIn users will not be able to find you when searching for you by name. This is also a violation of the LinkedIn User Agreement, and you don't want to lose your account.

☒ **Put anything in the picture area but a headshot picture of yourself.** No group pictures, no kids, no spouse, no logo. A professional photo is not required; just use a simple headshot picture from any standard digital camera. LinkedIn will help you crop it to the required 85 × 85 pixels.

☒ **Use the default descriptors for websites, such as My Company, My Website, and so forth.** Put a custom label in place of this text by selecting the "Other" option from the pull-down menu used to select the descriptor. It pops up a new field so that you can put in a custom label. It is okay to point to specific subpages on a website.

☒ Include only recent jobs, as you may be tempted to do. Put in all of your work history, back to college days. This gives you more inroads to create more relationships with others.

☒ Use paragraphs longer than five lines as they appear in the View My Profile section. Break up paragraphs with six or more lines into multiple paragraphs.

AHA! Zen Moment

How should you ACT on LinkedIn?

Attract: Create a compelling profile. Use LinkedIn groups to connect with others who might be good referral sources or potential joint venture partners.

Convert: Use the LinkedIn Answers feature to get strangers to consume your information and perhaps even turn into clients!

Transform: Get recommendations from your contacts on LinkedIn. This is a great way to showcase your expertise! 🧘

How to Be Proactive on LinkedIn

The following tips will help you use LinkedIn proactively.

- **Gain more visibility.** By adding connections, you further the likelihood that someone will find you when they need you. Write a compelling profile, and keep your contact database updated with your professional contacts.
- **Increase your rank with search engines.** LinkedIn allows you the option of making your profile public, which will allow search engines to index it. This is a very smart move, because LinkedIn is ranked very highly by search engines. When you create a public profile, select "Full View." Instead

of using the default URL LinkedIn provides, customize your public profile's URL to include your actual name.

- **Get business advice.** LinkedIn Answers are a great way to get advice and find answers to your most pressing questions. This is an especially useful tool if you are a business-to-business company.
- **Conduct market research.** I have done some excellent market research using the LinkedIn Answers feature. Not sure what your potential clients or customers feel their greatest need is? Just ask. Need to test out the market with a new idea? Ask for feedback. LinkedIn's Answers feature makes it easy.

> "In short, I think Google has a winner. Bugs and warts are easy to fix when the foundation is solid. Congratulations."
>
> Mike Loukides,
> *vice president of content strategy*
> *for O'Reilly Media, Inc.*

Google+
The Fastest Growing Social Networking Site

Why Bother With Google+?

- As of August 2011, it already had 25 million visitors (and it's still growing).
- It sees over 1 billion new shared and received items each day.
- *It has already signed up 13 percent of United States adults and plans on adding 9 percent more over the next year.*
- Its users include influential members of top media players such as Google, Apple, Microsoft, IBM, Infosys, and other companies.
- Its profile provides excellent visibility for you and your personal brand identity.
- Its "Circles" feature is a great way to form connections with users in all different industries and areas of expertise.

Google has a track record of producing popular projects that change the internet as we know it: a search engine, an email client, an advertising program, an internet browser, and much, much more. In late June 2011, Google added one of the most ambitious social projects so far to their already impressive creation portfolio: **Google+**.

This new social network is a multifaceted online experience that brings together innovative features such as friend streams, group video chat, personalized search feeds, and more. However, Google+ has *so many* new, exciting features that it can be confusing for those just starting out.

Luckily, this chapter will help you set up your Google+ profile and get the most out of this interactive online social experience.

Getting Started with Google+

Setting Up Your Google+ Profile

Just like with any other social networking site, the first step is setting up your profile, because your profile is key to your Google+ experience. Be sure to spend time crafting up a well-thought-out profile complete with an informative "About Me" section, relevant links to your online networks, and a photo that will help you stand out.

Google+ is easily accessed by logging into your Google account, then clicking on "+You" in the upper left corner of the navigation bar. You can also go directly to plus.Google.com. To create your profile, simply click on the profile button on the Google+ navigation bar:

Once you are at your profile page, click on the blue "Edit Profile" button in the upper-right-hand corner. You may then start to fill in any personal information that you wish to display in your profile, such as a brief introduction, your occupation and employment, personal hyperlinks, your education, a brief tagline, and more. Just as in your personal Facebook profile, you shouldn't share any information that has the potential to embarrass you.

AHA! Zen Moment

Be sure to optimize the links that you feature on the right side of your profile. Using specific, targeted SEO keywords will help Google value those links highly. 🧘

Before you save your profile, be sure that you turn on your search visibility, simply by checking the box that says, "Help others find my profile in search results," at the bottom of the page. This will not only help people find your profile but also alert Google to index your profile page.

Adding Contacts to Circles

One of Google+'s best-implemented features is Circles. This system allows you to organize all of your contacts into specific groups or categories: Friends, Family, Colleagues, College Buds, Acquaintances, or whatever group you prefer.

The idea behind Circles is that a social network should not be about sharing information with everyone but instead allow you to target specific social groups depending on what you want to share. For instance, if you are working on an impressive presentation at work, you may want to share this with your work colleagues but not your brother-in-law or your old college roommate. However, if you are uploading pictures from your BBQ last weekend, this is something that may not be particularly interesting to your boss or receptionist.

To add contacts to your Circles, simply head to the Circles tab at the top of the Google+ toolbar. From there, you can see who may have already added you to their Circles, add people to your Circles, or find and invite your own contacts from your personal email account.

Once you have imported all of your contacts, you can begin to drag and drop individuals into your personalized circles.

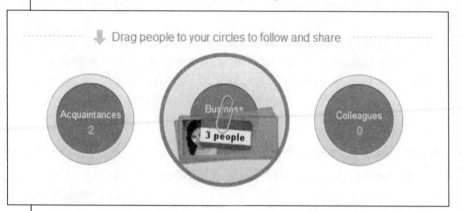

Managing Your Stream

The core of Google+ is your main Stream page. Similar to Google Buzz or the Facebook News Feed, the Google+ Stream is made up of content uploaded by your connections pictures, posts, links, location updates, videos, and other content. These updates refresh automatically and can be commented on or "+1"-ed (Google's version of the Facebook "Like" button) by followers.

On your main Stream page, there is also a list of your different Circles along the left-hand side of the stream. This allows you to switch back and forth between streams for different groups. You can also look at the "Incoming" stream, which features posts from people who have added you to their Circles, but whom you have not added to yours.

At the top of the Stream is the "Share What's New" box, which

lets you post and share content with your different Circles by selecting which Circles or people you'd like to share with at the bottom of the box (again, much like Facebook). However, if you are sharing information with one of your Circles that you would like to keep private, be sure to disable post resharing.

Setting Up Your Photos

Google has created a section of Google+ specifically for sharing, managing, and editing photos. This quick, well-organized editor allows users to tag photos that they have shared, then edit them to look more "artistic" and professional.

By clicking the "Photos" tab at the top of the Google+ bar, you will be taken to all of the photos that you have shared with your Circles, along with other photos that you have been tagged in.

Also, once you have Google+ added on your phone (as of this writing, it's only available for Android), you can automatically have your mobile photos uploaded to Google+ through the Instant Uploader feature.

Starting Hangouts

One of the most interesting aspects of Google+ is the Hangout feature. Hangouts are basically virtual chat rooms where you can video chat with people in your Circles. However, Google has added a few more features to make Hangouts more than just video chatting.

Instead of directly asking an individual to join you in a video chat, you instead click "Start A Hangout" on the right side of your Stream page.

Hangouts

Have fun with all your circles using your live webcam.

Start a hangout

A message goes out to your selected Circles, letting them know that you are interested in "hanging out." Once your connections begin to join your Hangout, the main video window will switch back and forth between people as they speak, moving faster as the group grows.

Image Source: Plus.Google.Com

Hangouts also allow you to watch YouTube videos with others in the group—the YouTube video appears in the main video window, and the individuals hanging out appear below—and text chat alongside the video windows.

Google+ Tricks and Shortcuts

Once you have set up your profile and previewed all of the exciting features that Google+ has to offer, you can start exploring the site and interacting with those in your Circles. Here are just a few useful tricks and shortcuts that you can use along the way to make your social experience just a little bit easier:

- **Text styling**: You can format the font in your posts by using the following tricks:
    - Including your text between *s will render the text bold. For example, *bold* will result in text that looks like this: **bold**.
    - Including your text between _s will render the text in italics. For example, _italics_ will result in a text that looks like this: *italics*.
    - Including your text between -s will strikethrough your text. For example, -strikethrough- will result in a text that looks like this: ~~strikethrough~~.

- **Keyboard shortcuts**: Google+ offers several shortcuts on the keyboard that make for easier navigation throughout the site:
  - Return Key = Begins your comment
  - Tab or Return Key = Ends your comment
  - Space Bar = Scrolls down your stream
  - Shift Key + Space Bar = Scrolls up your stream
  - J Key = Jumps down a single post on your stream
  - K Key = Jumps up a single post on your stream
  - Q Key = Jumps to chat
- **Private messaging**: Although Google+ does not currently feature a set way to private message other users, there is a simple trick that you can do to send a message to one, and only one, of your connections. Simply share a post with the required person instead of a Circle, then disable the re-sharing option. This will accomplish the same thing that a private message would.
- **Tagging users in posts**: You can tag anyone within your Circles in one of your posts simply by adding an @ or + before their name.
- **Using the +1 button**: Clicking the "+1" button on Google+ is essentially the same as clicking "Like" on a Facebook status update. In order to remove your +1, simply click the button again and it will be undone.
- **Searching**: To search through content on Google+, simply head to gplussearch.com, which allows you to search all public Google+ posts easily, much like the search bar on Twitter.

What Does Google+ Mean For Your Business?

Just as this book goes to print, Google+ has launched pages for businesses and brands.

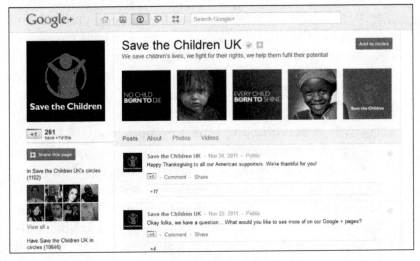

Here are five things you need to know about Google+ pages for businesses and brands:

1. **Pages are directly connected to Google search.** This is the feature that really sets Google+ pages apart from Facebook pages: the search integration. An advantage of a Google+ page is its integration with Google's web search function, and the ability to "direct connect." What does that mean? It means if a consumer wants to find a brand's Google+ page, all they have to do is type "+brandname" into Google to be taken directly to that page. Here is how Google recommends you connect them:

   To link your Google+ page and your website:

   1. Add the Google+ icon to your website
      To add the icon, just grab a snippet of code from here: https://developers.google.com/+/plugins/badge/config.

Paste it into your HTML code, and you're done: Your Google+ page and your site are now linked.

2. Link to your website from your Google+ Pages profile
For example, if you've created a page for a product, you can add the product description page to your page's profile. It's best to link to your home page or most significant page.

2. **Pages cannot switch or assign multiple administrators (yet).** If you're thinking of setting up a Google+ page for your brand, make sure the person who sets it up is the person you have (or want) in charge of your social media efforts. As of this writing, Google has not created a way to shift ownership of the page from one user to another. There also isn't the capability for multiple page administrators. Google has said that this is just temporary, but you'll still want to make sure that whoever has the initial responsibility for the page is the person you want to be updating the page.

3. **Practically anyone can set up a page.** Although the terms of service for a Google+ page state that they must be created by people "with authority over the subject matter," this still leaves plenty of room for duplicate pages, unofficial fan pages, or even fake brand pages. The general assumption is that Google will crack down on fake and duplicate pages, but they could also go the way Twitter did (they have official guidelines for parody and fan accounts).

4. **Pages have different options for local businesses/places.** Like Facebook fan pages, Google+ allows you to select a category for your page when you're first creating it. The options are similar no matter what you choose, with the exception of one: local business or place.

If your business is already in Google Places, all you have to do is type in your business phone number to get started.

If not, you have to add your business to Google Places first (although if you're tech-savvy enough to want to set up a Google+ page, this shouldn't take you very long). After you type in the phone number associated with your business, your physical location will show up as part of your new page.

5. **You can't add people to one of your Circles unless they add your brand page to one of their Circles first.** This is how Google makes sure that people can't be spammed by Google+ brand pages. When an individual adds you to one of their Circles, it gives you "permission" to add them to one of yours. (This is only true for brand pages on Google+. On your "personal" Google+ profile, you can add people to a Circle regardless of whether they've added you.)

Tips for Being Proactive on Google+

The following tips will help you to become more proactive on Google+ and form a better relationship with your followers:

- **Generate unique posts.** Although it can be very tempting to use Google+ to share the same information that you are posting on Twitter and Facebook, it is very likely that many people in your Google+ Circles are the same people that are your friends on Facebook and followers on Twitter. Therefore, you want to make sure that you are creating and posting fresh, original content uniquely for Google+, in order to generate quality traffic and user responses.

- **Share others' information that you are interested in.** Google+ makes it very easy to share news stories and photos from people in your Circles. Reposting this content is a great way to show your followers what you are interested in, and can also help establish you as an informant in whatever field you are posting about.

- **+1 postings that you enjoy.** While you show Facebook followers that you enjoy what they are posting by "liking" their content, you show interest in your Circles' postings by "+1"-ing them. This is also a great way to open the door to new connections and conversations with people that you may not know very well.

- **Manage your reputation.** Just as you should do with any other social networking site, it is important to monitor the content and information that you put out onto the web. If you are representing a company or brand through Google+, only post images and content that reflect positively on your image and company message.

Google+ Extensions for Google Chrome

Because Google+ is created completely by Google, it only makes sense that they would offer all of their outside extensions and applications through their native web browser Google Chrome. If you have this browser installed on your computer, here are just a few interesting add-ons that you can install to Chrome to enhance your Google+ experience:

- **Start Google+:** This Google Chrome extension offers complete social network integration between your Google+ account and other social networking sites. For instance, it allows you to combine your Facebook and Twitter streams with your Google+ stream. It also includes the option to post to these sites automatically whenever you share something on Google+.
- **+Photo zoom:** This simple extension for Google+ allows you to enlarge photos easily within your Google+ stream so that you can view the image more clearly. The best part of this application is that you do not need to click or open anything to make the image larger. Simply hovering over the images and profile pictures in your stream will enlarge them.
- **-1 (Minus One):** Since the very first day that Facebook created a "Like" button on their posts, users have been begging and pleading for a dislike button to complement their news

feed options. Google has implemented this option early on for Chrome users. The -1 application allows you to "-1" any of your friends' posts or updates...just to keep things even, of course.

- **Notification Count for Google+:** Just as the title states, this Google Chrome extension allows you to keep track of your Google+ notifications on your browser extension toolbar. Any unread notifications from your Google+ account will appear as a red numbered box right beside your search bar. Clicking this box will take you right to Google+ to view your notification and respond.

There's also a great Google+ application not for Chrome: **GClient**, a free desktop application that integrates Google+ into your Windows tray, allowing you to view your Google+ activities and notifications without ever leaving your desktop. It also allows you to post messages and follow the activities of your different circles.

What's Next for Google+?

Although Google+ already has a lot of great content and features, it is still in its beginning development stages and will continue to grow, adding new services as time goes on. It's obvious that Google also plans on combining this new social project with their many other services, given its core group of innovative projects and the new navigation bar atop all Google products that integrates its services.

For more Google+ tips and information, check out the article "10 Ways to Use Google+ for Marketing" on http://www.market-ingzen.com/10-ways-to-use-google-plus-for-marketing/. You can also follow my Google+ page at www.gplus.com/Shama for more Google+ tips to come.

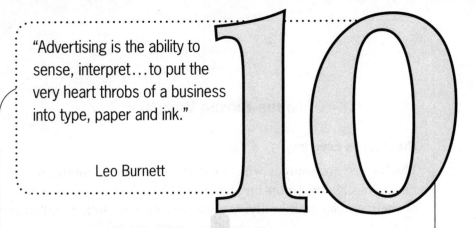

Social Advertising
Groupon, LivingSocial, and Facebook Ads…Oh My!

SIMPLY DEFINED, social advertising is all about using social networks to market to the individuals within them using context and relevancy. This category of advertising includes everything from group-buying sites like Groupon to the ads you see in your sidebar on Facebook.

Given that group-buying sites are all the rage recently, I thought it appropriate to briefly address how to best utilize them. I've asked good friend and colleague Albert Maruggi, founder and president of ProvidentPartners.net, to share his thoughts on what he calls the "buyer's economy." I first heard Albert speak of the "buyer's economy" during a webinar we copresented, and knew that it was the foundation for all social advertising.

At the end of the chapter, Albert has also included an introduction to using Facebook ads, because as of this writing, Facebook is one of the most popular and cost-effective mediums for advertising, social or otherwise.

Group-Buying Websites

The Buyer's Economy

The buyers' economy is what I call the purchasing environment made possible by group-buying sites, where buyers take control of their purchases by rallying members of their individual networks in pursuit of a deeply discounted product or service. It requires a combination of the following: deep discount, limited time, and a qualifying quantity of customers who must purchase the deal for everyone to benefit.

Most people today are familiar with group-buying sites because of the success of Groupon (www.groupon.com) and its biggest competitor, LivingSocial (www.livingsocial.com). Like other group-buying sites, they partner with a variety of different types of companies to provide discounts on products and services, both locally and nationally. These deals run for a short amount of time, rarely longer than a few days.

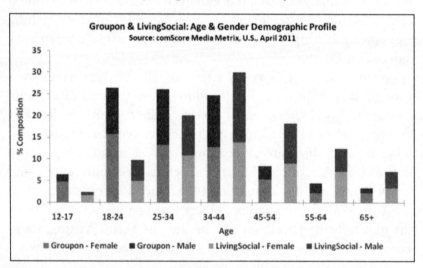

Comparative demographic data for Groupon and LivingSocial. Check ComScore.com for any updated studies.

Why should marketers bother with these sites? For starters, Groupon alone has 85 million users (and counting). Its users are generally between the ages of 18 and 44, and also tend to be slightly better educated than the average users of other social networks. It can also be a great way to market your business—provided that your business is a good match for what group-buying sites have to offer.

How Group-Buying Sites Work

The basic premise of the group-buying site is that a company offers a deal—say, get a $50 restaurant voucher for only $25, or six yoga classes for the price of three—in exchange for some percentage of what site users are asked to pay to receive it. There are no set rules on the type of deals included or the percentage the company receives; each offer is negotiated individually.

Customers sign up to receive these deals by registering with a valid email address, either on the company's website or through an app downloaded onto a smartphone. Customers do not have to register simply to view the deals for the day, but they do have to register if they'd like to purchase any.

If a required minimum number of people are interested in what a company has to offer, the deal happens; if not enough people are interested, then the deal is off.

Customers can see the minimum number of people required, and whether that number has been reached. If it hasn't, customers can encourage their friends to buy the deal and increase the chances of "tipping the scale" (the term Groupon uses). Customers are also rewarded by engaging their own social networks: when a customer refers friends to group-buying sites, he or she is often rewarded with extra discounts and other "goodies."

The Benefits of Group-Buying Sites

This setup obviously benefits both the customer and the group-buying site. The customer gets a deeply discounted product, and the site gets a cut of what the customer pays. But where's the payoff for the businesses involved?

Offering deals on group-buying sites actually pays off in three different ways:

- **It provides exposure.** Eighty-five million potential customers is nothing to turn up your nose at (of course, that's counting users in all cities and regions). The point is, these sites are a great source for finding new customers. Even if a customer who sees your deal isn't interested in purchasing something from you immediately, they're still seeing your company's name. Even if your deal doesn't happen, you've still received great advertising. And it's a great opportunity not just to meet new customers but also to reconnect with established customers. Chances are that some of your current customers are subscribers to group-buying sites.
- **It drives customers into stores, online and off.** A group-buying site brings people into your store, whether that store is brick and mortar or css and html, increasing their exposure to your company and your products. Once there, you can provide them with an amazing experience they want to

share with their friend networks. They might spend more than the amount of the group-buying deal—or come back again to make other purchases in the future.

- **It's a performance-based expense.** Offering a group-buying deal is low in risk. Businesses get to negotiate the minimum number of customers that have to buy the deal before it becomes active, so if the costs outweigh the benefits at less than a certain number of customers, you can set the minimum number higher. You can also ask for a ceiling on the number of deals available for purchase, giving your business a cap on the total amount the program will cost. Plus, if the deal doesn't go through, you haven't lost any money. At worst, you've still gained a lot of free advertising.

Is Your Company a Good Match for Group Buying?

Yes! Or probably yes because the model is so flexible. No matter what kind of product or service you offer, there's probably a way you can use group-buying sites to increase your customer base. However, there are a number of considerations to take into account before you jump in.

- **Will offering a group-buying deal be financially worthwhile?** Choosing to go with a group-buying site because you're in a blind panic for more customers is absolutely the wrong way to do things. You need to research your options and pick the site, and the type of deal, that's right for your company. This will take a little bit of time and shouldn't be rushed. Look at the pros and cons. Compare financial compensation plans.

  A social buying network's cut can be anywhere from 15 to 50 percent, making the true cost of business to the company offering the deal up to 75 percent of the purchase price. Make sure such a cost is a worthwhile one for your business. I've put together a return on investment (ROI) form for a fictional restaurant as an example.

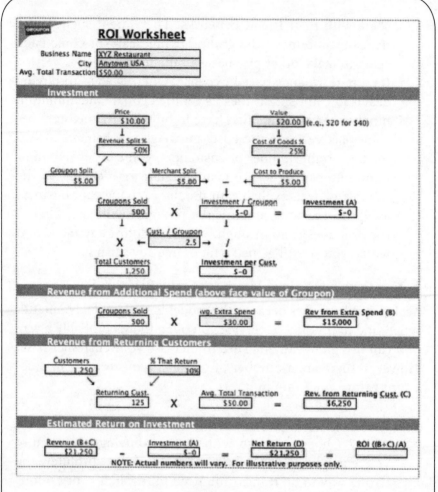

ROI Worksheet

Business Name XYZ Restaurant
City Anytown USA
Avg. Total Transaction $50.00

Investment

Price $10.00
Value $20.00 (e.g., $20 for $40)

Revenue Split % 50%
Cost of Goods % 25%

Groupon Split $5.00
Merchant Split $5.00 — − ← Cost to Produce $5.00

Groupons Sold 500 X Investment / Groupon $-0 = Investment (A) $-0

X ← Cust. / Groupon 2.5 → /

Total Customers 1,250
Investment per Cust. $-0

Revenue from Additional Spend (above face value of Groupon)

Groupons Sold 500 X Avg. Extra Spend $30.00 = Rev from Extra Spend (B) $15,000

Revenue from Returning Customers

Customers 1,250
% That Return 10%

Returning Cust. 125 X Avg. Total Transaction $50.00 = Rev. from Returning Cust. (C) $6,250

Estimated Return on Investment

Revenue (B+C) $21,250 − Investment (A) $-0 = Net Return (D) $21,250 = ROI ((B+C)/A)

NOTE: Actual numbers will vary. For illustrative purposes only.

Consider also how many people will see your offer even if it doesn't end up going into effect. Ask those in charge of the group-buying sites you're considering working with about the number of subscribers in your geographical area.

- **Is your product or service perishable or cyclical?** Products and services with a limited lifespan (like food or flowers) or which are available in specific quantities at any given time (like hotel rooms or spa treatments) are especially well suited to group-buying sites. The extra customers who visit your hotel through a group-buying site are buying rooms at a discount that might normally have remained empty; customers at your flower shop are buying flowers at a discount that normally might have gone to waste.

- **Are price-sensitive buyers your ideal customers?** Group-buying customers tend to be deal seekers—they may only spend the Groupon amount and not more, and may not come back again. If you're looking to create repeat business, this is obviously not an ideal situation. Ask yourself if any of your regular-priced goods and services are appealing enough (read: cheap enough) to make the group-buying subscriber want to make the jump to regular customer.
- **Can your company's cash flow handle the group-buying reimbursement model?** Different group-buying sites have different ways of reimbursing you, and rarely is it quick or all at once. Although LivingSocial usually reimburses a business within 15 days of the end of a deal, Groupon can take up to three months—which can be less than ideal for a small business or restaurant, or anyone who needs to make up the costs of the group-buying program in a timely fashion. Make sure your business is prepared.

How to Use Group-Buying Sites Effectively

If you've decided group buying is the right choice for you and your company, you need to make sure to take full advantage of the opportunities in front of you. Here are some ways to make sure you're using group buying and social advertising to the fullest extent possible:

- **Negotiate.** The standard commission rate for both Groupon and LivingSocial is about 50 percent…unless you negotiate. Keep in mind that these websites have a ton of competitors (and there are more of them every day), so it's becoming easier and easier to negotiate a mutually beneficial arrangement.
- **Make group-buying customers your customers.** Unless customers who buy your deal provide you with an email

> The killer was email address acquisition . . . We converted approximately 25 percent of in store redemptions into signing up for our email list . . . which is on track to generate an additional five to six figures in online revenue.
>
> ### American Apparel,
> *[Source: Business Insider Groupon website]*

address or some other means of contacting them, they're really the group-buying site's customers, not yours. But you can change that. In your promotional copy, provide a link back to a landing page on your website where customers can provide you with their email addresses. Even if they don't want to buy your offer, they still might want to sign up for a newsletter and keep you on their radar (which is definitely a step in the right direction). Also provide links to all your other social platforms.

You also can acknowledge group-buying customers specifically on your website or store premises, whether through a sign or graphic welcoming LivingSocial customers or a special night set aside just for Groupon customers. This provides a way for you to communicate specifically with the group-buying customer and pass on important information—for example, that you're on Yelp and they should leave you a review (or to check out your Facebook and Twitter sites).

- **Provide a bridge from the discounted deal price to full-price items.** Going from paying a discounted price to paying full price is not always a natural transition, so anything you can do to help that process is beneficial. If you use one of your signature items—for example, your most popular entrée or a smaller version of it—in the group-buying offer, consider also providing samples of other premium price items for those customers, to encourage them to return and pay full price another time.

- **Remember to upsell and cross-sell.** In the past, many participants of group-buying sites have found that customers are reluctant to spend more than the value of the coupon. This is where you have to put in some more effort. If you're a restaurant, make sure your staff is consistently suggesting additional items: cocktails, side dishes, desserts, and other menu items. Hotel? See if guests want to upgrade their rooms for a small fee upon check-in. With a little (and we mean *little*) push, some of these customers will be willing to spend a few extra dollars with you.
- **Make sure you provide the best service possible.** People who are active on group-buying sites are also likely to be very active users of other social media sites. If your service is less than top-notch when they come to redeem their discount, be assured that their entire network of friends will hear all about it. This may sound obvious, but it's something many business owners overlook. The first rule of using a social buying network is to get your house in order, from product to service to decor to staff, and make sure everyone responsible for the customer experience understands the social buying customer. If you deliver average, you'll get average comments online. People will not go out of their way for average. This point needs to be reinforced at every staff meeting prior to and during the deal redemption period.

  Although group-buying sites don't come without their share of potential downfalls for you and your business, they also have a lot of potential. Your experience with these sites, much like your experience with any other social site, depends on how you use it. If you do your homework and provide great service to your customers, then you'll see the benefits.

Some quick tips for using social buying networks profitably:

- Double check financial formulas and work toward the most profitable outcome.
- Create a way for social network buyers to provide their email addresses to you, whether by using a unique landing page for each group-buying program to capture email addresses or by encouraging group-buying customers to sign up when they come to redeem their deal.
- Provide all other social platforms your business is involved in landing pages and, if possible, in the social buying network copy to increase your number of followers.
- Print signage, decals, or some other visual reminder of your other social platforms, which will be mental hints for customers to share their experience.
- Identify and plan for offering potential upsells and cross-sells.
- Invite buyers to communicate directly with you to help make their experience favorable. 🧘

Facebook Advertising

Facebook's advertising program gives you the ability to place an ad, sponsored story, or post on the right side of a user's page. It's one of the most customizable advertising platforms for business, one in which the business can quickly determine whether their message and audience are connecting. In some cases, Facebook ads even show users which of their friends have already liked the particular product or service—combining the power of traditional advertising with word-of-mouth appeal.

Advertising on Facebook has a variety of advantages:

- It allows you to target your audience by interests, geography, and age, and quantifies audience size.

- You get immediate feedback on how well your message and audience criteria are working.
- You can easily drive traffic to your Facebook fan page or company website.

The big downside to advertising on Facebook is that Facebook is not Google (obviously): people aren't on Facebook to search for something specific, they're there to connect with their friends and family. Facebook is not traditionally a shopping platform; people are not generally on Facebook to shop. Users connect with brands and "like" pages of companies, but those are connections based on experience or association with the company or with others in their network.

How to Use Facebook Advertising Effectively

Each company and customer base is different, and the social web changes too rapidly for hard and fast rules. Still, we can offer some guidelines to help you get started in setting up an ad. The following ideas may help you find a strategy for using Facebook advertising that works for your business.

The key to Facebook advertising is making sure you understand your customer. This will determine which Facebook users you target, and also the content of your ad.

For this section, we'll use the example of a bakery with three different target audiences: college students, parents with young children, and people living within a certain distance of the store. Getting these three groups of people to a bakery means using three different types of ads. So let's focus on just one of these audiences: college students.

The first step to creating an effective Facebook ad is to write down the attributes of the types of customers best suited to your products or services. Most undergraduate college students are between the ages of eighteen and twenty-four. What else do we know about college students? They spend a lot of time studying, they generally don't have a lot of money, and they stay up late.

The next step is actually to set up your ad, which involves entering several key pieces of information.

- **Targeting**: The Targeting section allows you to determine the size of your potential audience based on the attributes of your customers. As you select the variables in this area (location, relationship status, age, gender, interests, religion, etc.), watch the Estimated Reach box to get a sense of the number of people that match your criteria. These are not precise numbers, but they do provide a starting point for whether to advertise—for example, if your estimated reach is 25 people, maybe it wouldn't be worth targeting that particular group. It also helps you understand what percentage capture of that audience is necessary for the ad to be successful.

  Our bakery could choose to target every person between 18 and 24 years old in a 10-mile radius of the physical shop. Or they could get even more precise and choose to target people in that age range that have a specific nearby university listed under their "education" section.

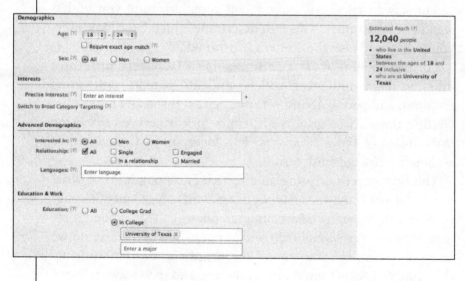

- **Content:** On Facebook, your ad content needs to be less about you and more about the customer. The most effective ads typically include four things:

  1. A provocative headline
  2. An emotional connection
  3. An offer or call to action
  4. An image that is memorable or involves faces

In our bakery example, a headline targeting college students could say, "All Studied Out?" or maybe, "Need to Escape the Library?" This taps into college students' personal experience; it's easy for them to connect with. You could then promote a special offer for students who come in after 5 PM: show a student I.D. to get a discount or a free drink. For an image, you could use a photo of a miserable-looking student reading a textbook—or a picture of a delicious-looking cupcake.

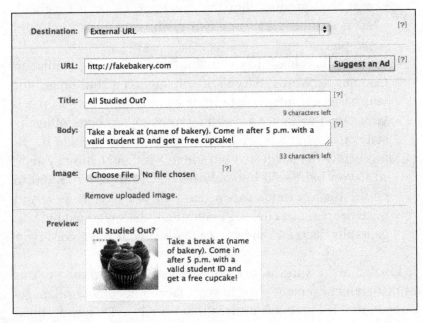

- **Budget:** Facebook gives you two options to pay for advertising: pay per click (PPC) or per thousand impressions (PPM).
  - With PPC, you are only charged when people click on your ads. This can end up being cheaper in the long run, especially when first testing the waters with Facebook ads. PPC is also a good pick for those on smaller budgets.
  - With PPM, you are charged for every thousand people who view the ad, whether they click on it or not. Paying for impressions usually costs less in the bid process, but this method often ends up costing more in the long run.

    Another term you should be familiar with here is click-through rate or CTR. Your CTR determines how much and how often you'll be charged if you choose PPC. It's also important because Facebook monitors your CTR and will run your ad less often if your rate is much lower than average. Your ad's display rate increases as the CTR increases. A good CTR varies depending on platform, format, and product, but the average CTR on a Facebook ad is around 0.25% (or two to three of every thousand people).
- **Bidding:** Facebook has you "bid" for keywords, similar to Google's AdWords. Facebook will suggest a "bid range" for you based on how much other companies trying to reach your target audience are willing to pay. (Facebook officially states that your ads are less likely to run on the site if you bid below the suggested bid range.) It's an auction system, so if you bid $1.00 but only needed to have bid $0.60 to be the highest bidder, then that's all you have to pay. And once people start clicking on your ad, the suggested bid will generally decrease, and you can adjust your bid accordingly.

Finally, make sure to monitor your ad results through your campaign management page, at www.facebook.com/ads/manage/campaigns/. If Facebook notices that an ad's CTR has declined

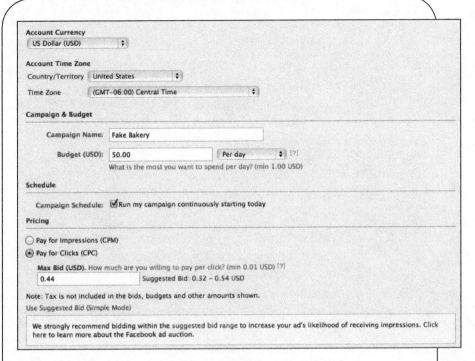

or isn't very high, they'll run the ad less often. It's important to monitor how your ad is doing. If you're not getting a very good response, change your strategy. You could target using different criteria or to a different group altogether. Try changing your headline; maybe it isn't compelling.

Although this may seem complicated or like a lot to take on, it's really not. Facebook wants you to advertise with them—let's face it, they want some of your money—and they help you as much as possible every step of the way. As we've said in previous chapters, Facebook is where the people are. You should be there too.

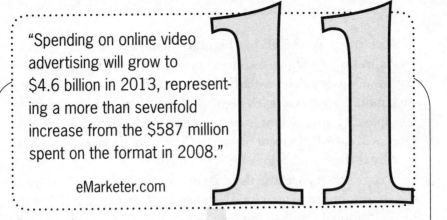

"Spending on online video advertising will grow to $4.6 billion in 2013, representing a more than sevenfold increase from the $587 million spent on the format in 2008."

eMarketer.com

Video
The Most Powerful Social Medium

ALTHOUGH VIDEO doesn't usually fall within the category of social networking sites, it is an important tool within the bigger sphere of online marketing. You can take the online video you create and share it across the board from your own blog to social networking sites. If content is king, video is the king of the bigger country.

My #1 source for online video information is Dave Kaminski of Web Video University (www.WebVideoUniversity.com). Dave teaches thousands of people online how to create successful online videos through his training programs. He is the expert when it comes to this area, so I have asked him to write this guest chapter.

In February 2005, three men launched a new website. In November 2006, Google bought that website for $1.65 billion. The website was called YouTube. Thus began the phenomenon of web video.

Since then, web video has become the fastest-growing form of media in history. Eighty-two percent of internet users (and growing) watch web video regularly. Almost 8 billion videos are viewed each month across Google's network. More than 40 hours of video are uploaded to YouTube every minute. And Cisco predicts that video will drive 80 percent of web traffic within the next four years.

Why is there such a love for web video?

In large part it's because that vast majority of people, when given the choice, prefer to watch rather than read. In fact, a 2007 study by the National Endowment for the Arts reports that "on average, Americans aged 15 to 24 spend almost two hours a day watching TV, and only seven minutes of their daily leisure time on reading." And you can bet that web video is only further fueling this difference in time spent watching versus reading across all age groups.

But what does all this mean for you, the website owner, business owner, blogger, or online marketer? What's the most effective way to use web video for your business? And how can you get started with web video, not only if the technology confounds you, but also if you've never touched a camera in your life?

I share the answers with you here. Answers that aren't based on theory, hearsay, or speculation, but rather on the real-world results of people who are earning their incomes, in full or in part, through web video.

Crafted intelligently, web video is a brilliant viral tool to attract, engage, and convert viewers to take action better than any other marketing medium on the web.

Sherman Hu,
ShermanLive.com

Of course there are lots of ways you can make web videos: you can record what you're doing on your screen, piece together videos using nothing but photos and stock footage, or turn the camera on yourself and star in your own videos.

But whatever you do, you're going to need some tools to create those videos. So to start, we're going to cover...

The Equipment You Need to Create Web Videos

This is often the most boring part of web video. However, it's also the part where people tend to have the most questions. Specifically, they want to know what equipment is the best.

My answer may surprise you. That's because when it comes to video equipment, there is no "best"—no best camera, no best microphone, and no best software. In the world of video, best is really a matter of opinion.

There are, however, certain guidelines you can and should follow—guidelines that will save you plenty of time, money, and headaches. And it's these guidelines that I'll be sharing with you here.

We'll start with video cameras first.

Virtually any video camera you buy these days will produce video that's of high enough quality for the web—even a $150 Flip camera. That doesn't mean you're going to get gorgeous, vibrant, broadcast-quality video—not even close. But your footage will be good enough.

If you want higher quality, you're going to have to spend more on a camera. With video cameras, you truly get what you pay for.

Personally, I recommend cameras from Canon's VIXIA line but Sony and Panasonic cameras are often just as good. In fact, if you were to go out and buy a camera today, I'd recommend you get a model from Canon, Sony, or Panasonic. As a rule, cameras from any of these three manufacturers will give you the best quality with the fewest headaches.

No matter what camera you choose, you'll want to make sure it comes with an external microphone jack. This jack will allow you to plug a microphone into your camera—for example, a lavalier microphone—which you can then attach to the front of your shirt. If you use an external microphone like this, the audio portion of your video will sound dramatically better than if you had used your camera's built-in microphone. In fact, this simple tip alone can dramatically increase the entire production value of your video.

Along the way, you're also going to be hit with the question of...

Should You Use High Definition or Standard Definition Video?

First, understand that, whether you use HD or SD video, it's still just video. The difference is that HD uses a lot more pixels, which means a sharper and more detailed image.

That better image comes at a price, though. To edit most HD video and get it ready to go on the web, you'll need a powerful computer—one with a multicore processor and at least 4 GB of memory.

Unfortunately, nearly every camera these days shoots in HD. Which means you may have no choice but to use HD video. Standard definition video is simply a technology that is on its way out.

Just understand that from a business standpoint, there is no advantage or disadvantage to using HD rather than SD video. It's still just video. And the only thing you gain with HD is a nicer-looking image.

No matter what type of format you shoot your videos in, you are still going to have to cut out portions of the video where you make mistakes, or maybe you'll want to add text, graphics, or background music to your videos.

So here's...

What You Need to Know About Video Editing Software

There are plenty of video editing software packages available. Windows comes with a free package called Movie Maker. Apple comes with iMovie. There are also inexpensive solutions available from Pinnacle, Ulead, Adobe, and others. But there are only two software packages that I recommend to people: for PC, Sony's Vegas (www.SonyCreativeSoftware.com), and for Mac, Apple's Final Cut (www.Apple.com/FinalCutExpress).

Why these two out of all the options available? Ease of use, affordability, and flexibility. Both Vegas and Final Cut offer beginner versions on which you can cut your teeth editing video for a low cost. Then, as your skills progress and you start wanting to do more with your video, you can upgrade to more advanced versions of these programs (all the way up to professional versions used to create Hollywood movies and TV shows). And when you do upgrade, you won't need to relearn the software. It's the same software with additional features.

With virtually all other video editing programs available, it's the opposite. They either don't offer an upgrade path or, if they do, they require you to learn a completely new (and confusing) software interface.

But what if you don't want to shoot live video? What if instead you want to record PowerPoint presentations or something you're doing on your computer screen? For this, you will need screen recording software.

My Recommendations for Screen Recording Software

First, let's discuss the difference between screen recording software and video editing software.

Screen recording software allows you to record movement on your computer screen, from demonstrations or tutorials on software to slide-based presentations. Video editing software allows you to take footage from a video camera, stock video clips, or even photos and edit everything in an unlimited number of ways—you're limited only by your imagination.

Video editing software cannot record your computer screen. And screen recording software is not designed to edit live footage from a camera.

When it comes to what software you should use if you want to record something on your screen, again, I have two recommendations. For PC, I recommend Camtasia from TechSmith (www.TechSmith.com). For Mac, I recommend ScreenFlow from Telestream (www.Telestream.net).

Although there are multiple competing programs available for each platform, these two are the runaway winners. You cannot go wrong with either of them.

There are also free and inexpensive web-based screen recording solutions available. The most popular and widely used is Jing (jingproject.com).

Now you know, at least on a basic level, the equipment you should use to create your videos. But that's only part of the battle. You still need to create your videos in such a way that viewers won't get bored and bolt after a few seconds.

Three Big Secrets for Making Sure People Watch Your Videos from Beginning to End

Many people mistakenly think that simply creating a video and putting it online means that everyone who comes across that video will watch it from start to finish.

Unfortunately, statistics paint a far different picture. Here's a look at viewer habits, as reported by the video distribution service TubeMogul:

- Within the first 10 seconds of a video, 10.39 percent of viewers are gone.
- Within the first 30 seconds of a video, 33.84 percent of viewers are gone.
- By the one-minute mark of a video, 53.56 percent of viewers are gone.
- By the two-minute mark of a video, 76.29 percent of viewers are gone.

In other words, the web video viewing community has a serious case of attention deficit disorder. To combat that and help hold the viewer's interest from beginning to end, there are three things we can do.

First is to regulate video length. Ideally, you want your web videos to be no more than two minutes in length. When you go beyond that, the number of viewers who click away increases dramatically. This doesn't mean your video has to be exactly two minutes long. However, you do want to keep that two-minute goal in your head. Follow this rule, and the odds of getting your complete message across to people will increase dramatically.

Second is to keep things moving. Watch any TV commercial, TV show, or movie. You'll notice that about every two to three seconds what you're seeing on the screen changes. There will be a different camera angle, a different scene, or a different image shown. And this happens repeatedly throughout the entire program. What you see is constantly moving and changing.

We've all watched enough television to have our brains programmed by this. If a scene remains static on the screen for too long—even just 10 seconds—we start to get bored and anxious.

In the world of web video, that's when people start clicking away from your video and onto something else. But by keeping things moving (which means avoiding static scenes of 10 seconds or more), you help keep viewers interested. It's a subtle but effective trick.

The third (and perhaps most important) technique is transparency—giving your viewer a behind-the-scenes look at your life or business. Or to put it another way, *being real*.

When web video first started heating up, advertisers repurposed their television commercials for the web. That means they took commercials that had been running on TV and stuck them as-is on the web. The results were disastrous. Turns out people on the web don't want to see TV-style videos. Why? Because the web is a social tool. People use it to connect with others. They don't want to see stiff, contrived, corporate-style presentations; they want to see real people. Which is exactly what transparency gives them.

What Shama does with her videos on Shama.TV is a perfect example of transparency in action. Watch her videos, and you will see that she's not on a fake set or in front of a green screen with a fake background superimposed. Instead, she's at her desk. Or on her couch. Or walking around her neighborhood. Or with her dog, Snoopy. She shares what she's reading, what she learned at a seminar, or even what someone may have sent her in the mail. The end result is that she comes across not only as a trustworthy authority but as someone who is genuine, approachable, and real.

And that's the idea behind transparency. Use it with video, and both your audience and business will grow.

But, of course, people have to see your videos first. And that's what we're going to cover next...how to get traffic and build an audience with web video. Let's start with...

What You Need to Know About Video Sharing Sites

When most people hear the words "web video," they instantly think of YouTube. YouTube, Viddler, Vimeo, Veoh, Blip.TV, Dailymotion, Metacafe, Revver, and a host of others are video sharing sites.

Most people are led to believe that by using video sharing sites, they'll gain a flood of traffic, sudden success, and maybe even instant stardom. Unfortunately, that couldn't be further from the truth. In fact, 53 percent of the videos on YouTube achieve fewer than 500 views, and 30 percent get less than 100 views. So I'll tell it to you straight without mincing any words: posting your videos on video sharing sites should only be used to get ancillary traffic, not primary traffic. There's actually a far, far better way to get traffic with web video, which I discuss later in this section.

First, let's cover how search engines like Google view and index videos. Actually, search engines (for the most part) don't view videos at all. Nearly all web videos are Flash files, and Flash files are more or less invisible to search engines. This means the content of a video isn't being viewed, indexed, and ranked by a search engine but rather the webpage a video is on is viewed, indexed, and ranked. Or, to put it another way, when you upload a video to a sharing site or place a video on your own webpage, search engines know a video is there, but they don't have any idea what that video contains. (Note: This is slowly changing as search engines learn to adapt.)

Search engines do look at the other items on a webpage—blog post titles, page titles, text on the page, incoming links, HTML tags, and so on—and that's how they figure out what a page is about. Again, the actual content in the video is ignored.

So how do you get people to find your videos, and how do you get them to appear in search engines? In the case of video sharing sites, you have to focus on metadata. I know that sounds like a "techie" word, but all it really means is the title, description, and tags you enter when uploading a video.

For example, when you upload a video to YouTube, you are asked to give the video a title, write a description about it, and enter a few tags (words that relate to the video's content). This is your metadata. And what you enter here will determine how your video shows up in search engine results and within the YouTube search results. So when writing your video title, description, and tags, you'll want to target the specific keywords that relate to your video. The following image shows an example of a video upload form with fields for metadata.

A few services are available that will allow you to upload your

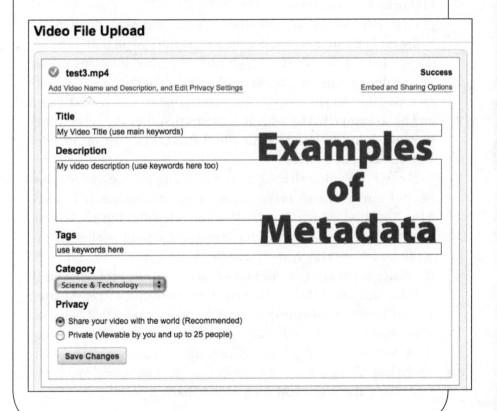

videos to multiple video sharing sites at once. This means that instead of going to each video sharing site individually and uploading your video, you only have to upload your video once, and it is automatically distributed across multiple sharing sites for you. The most popular of these services is TubeMogul (TubeMogul. com). It also happens to be free. When using a service like Tube-Mogul, you will be asked to enter metadata for your video...and that metadata will be used for every sharing site TubeMogul distributes your video to.

Sounds pretty good, doesn't it? You've got all these free video sharing sites and a free distribution service like TubeMogul, where with just a few clicks your videos instantly appear across multiple sites.

So why in the world would I tell you to use video sharing sites only for ancillary traffic? There are a number of reasons, but I'll highlight the most important.

First, remember that with video, it is the webpage it's on that is being ranked and indexed, not the actual video. And that webpage doesn't belong to you; it belongs to the sharing site. This means your videos are driving traffic to the video sharing site, not your own website. To get to your site, viewers must watch your video and be so compelled by what it contains that they stop everything they are doing and go to your site instead. The vast majority of viewers will not do this.

Second, all video sharing sites are losing money. No one has figured out a way to make money from user-generated video. Even YouTube, which dwarfs all other video sharing sites, is rumored to be just reaching the break-even point—after losing millions for several years. (Google doesn't reveal YouTube's financials, but analysts unanimously agree it's not profitable yet.)

What this means for you is that at any moment, a video sharing site can go out of business and close its doors. And if that happens, your videos (and any traffic they may generate) will disappear, too.

Just in case you think something like this can't happen, it already has. Google has shut down Google Video, and AOL and MSN have also closed off their video-sharing portals.

Finally, there's a far better way to generate traffic and build an audience through web video. A way that lets you retain total control and ownership of your videos. A way that lets you easily generate top Google rankings for your videos. And a way that allows all the traffic you generate to go directly to your own site.

Let me introduce you to...

The Power of Video Podcasting

When you throw around the word "podcast," most people knowingly nod their heads but are secretly baffled by the term. And when you add the word "video," things get even more confusing.

So first let me define what a video podcast is. In technical terms, it's a series of videos released episodically and distributed through RSS and downloaded by viewers through syndication channels.

In simpler terms, it's usually a blog that contains all video. These videos focus on a particular topic and contain pure content (no sales pitches). They are delivered once a day, every other day, or once a week. And the built-in RSS feed for the blog can distribute these videos directly to people's email boxes, other websites, and services such as iTunes.

It's automatic, free syndication for your videos.

For example, let's say you love to bake, so you start a video podcast on how to bake cookies, cakes, and other treats. One week you create a video on baking apple pie. The next week you create a video on baking chocolate chip cookies. The next week it's cupcakes. And you continue on producing episodic videos like these each week.

Because your videos are on a website you own (again, usually a blog), all the traffic your videos generate goes directly to you. In addition, your video podcast can be picked up, via RSS feed, by multiple podcast directories, which search engines love. Why do search engines love podcast directories? Because they are *authority sites* on the internet. They receive large amounts of traffic; contain relevant, human-reviewed content; and are awarded high

PageRank by Google. For you, this means a video listed in a pod-cast directory can rank higher in the search engines than the same video on a sharing site.

But it gets better. Your video podcast can also be distributed to huge networks like iTunes, Zune, and Miro. And if that isn't enough, you can *still* take each of your podcast videos and upload them to sharing sites, too, for ancillary traffic.

Though all this usually sounds intriguing to people, they are often still not convinced about this whole podcasting thing. So let me give you some proof. I conducted a head-to-head comparison of a podcasted video and the same video uploaded to YouTube. For this comparison I created a video in which I reviewed the perfor-mance of a particular piece of software. This video was posted on my podcast site. The same video was uploaded to YouTube. I used identical metadata (title, description, tags) for both my podcast site and YouTube.

A few days later, I Googled the title of my video. The following image shows the results.

As you can see, both the YouTube video and my podcast site video were listed in the middle of the first page of results, side by side. So we're all even at this point, right? Not exactly.

First, you have to ask yourself if you'd rather have someone click on a link that takes him to YouTube or a link that takes him to your own site. I think all of us would rather have that traffic go to our own site, and that's exactly what podcast video accomplishes.

Why do these podcast videos perform so well in the search engines, even when going head-to-head with similar content on giants like YouTube? No one knows for sure about the inner workings of search engines and the complex algorithms they use. However, it's suspected that Google favors both blogs and video content. And with video podcasting, we're using both.

In addition, because videos are distributed via RSS feeds, they can instantly appear on multiple websites, which often link back to your website. And the more relevant links you have pointing

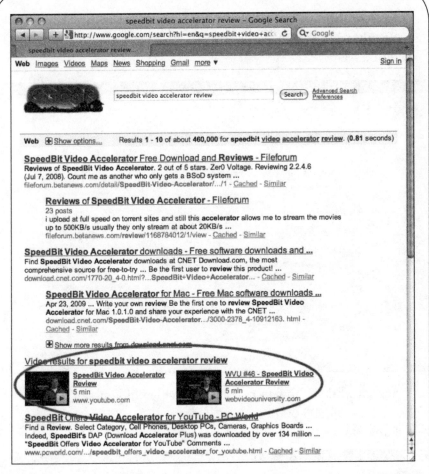

to your website, the higher your site can rank with the search engines. This means that through video podcasting, we are able to target specific keywords for a market and can often rank higher for those keywords than we would through traditional SEO techniques.

But let's look at two more examples of the power of video podcasting in action.

For these examples, I went to my own podcast site (WebVideoUniversity.com/podcast) and Shama's podcast site (Shama.TV). I noted a few of the video titles from each and Googled them. Here are the results:

Search phrase: how to create the ultimate business card
Results: 342,000,000
Rank: #1

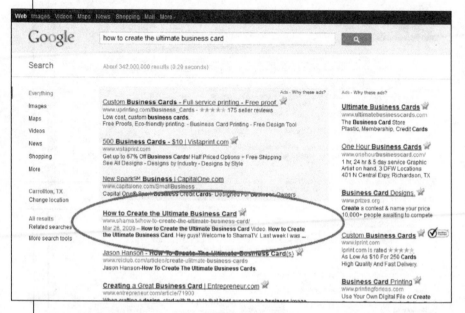

Search phrase: how to make a twin video of yourself
Results: 39,300,000
Rank: #1

Keep in mind—these videos were originally posted *over two years ago*. Yet they've retained their top positions, among tens of millions of competing pages, for all that time.

Are There Any Drawbacks to Doing a Video Podcast?

Yes. Running a video podcast takes passion, commitment, and dedication. You have to continually produce videos on a set schedule (daily, weekly, etc.), and you have to make sure the content is always fresh, relevant, and useful. Do that, and you can achieve the same results that Shama and I and many, many others have.

However, if you roar out of the gate only to give up a month later (which a lot of people do), you obviously won't get the same results, if any. You can still post videos now and then to your site, and you may pick up some rankings for them, but you won't build traffic or an audience nearly as effectively as you can with a video podcast.

Of course, as we discuss in the next section, there are many things you can do with web video beyond just podcasts. Here are...

Two of the Most Lucrative Ways to Use Web Video

One lucrative way to use web video is product creation, as in using web video to create products. There are a number of ways you can do this, from screen recordings that demonstrate software to screen recordings that teach a particular topic to live videos that teach or demonstrate a topic to combinations of both. Video has a much higher perceived value than printed material. For example, an ebook that sells for $29 can carry a price of $49 or higher in video form.

Video products can also be a lot faster to create than printed material. Whereas it may take several weeks or months to create printed training materials, that same training in video form often takes just several days. In fact, I've created numerous video products for both myself and clients over a single weekend. In the old days, when everything was 100 percent written, it would have taken me months.

But there's another ancillary benefit of developing web video skills. And it addresses a market that could not be any more wide open. What's the market? Creating videos for other website owners. I call it *web video consulting*.

There are billions of websites on the internet. Obviously, not all of the sites are business-related, and not all of the website owners want video. But there is a vast market in which sites are business-related, the owners want video, and they want someone to do it for them. The problem is that there are not enough people out there who can provide these services for them. But for those who can, it can be a very lucrative proposition.

For example, the average cost to have a web video professionally shot, edited, and produced is $3,000. That's just for the video. What if the client wants help with video SEO, website design, or marketing? Those are all value-added services that you can provide for additional fees.

The market is definitely out there and waiting if you're willing to go after it. I have students who right now are actively earning the fees I describe. And some even have to turn away work because they are so booked.

But perhaps an even more compelling reason for developing video skills is...

The Future of Web Video

Right now when we watch web video either for entertainment or education, we sit down at our computers to do it or we watch on our phones and tablet devices. But in the not so distant future, we will be watching much of it directly from our TVs too. In fact, it already has a name: *IPTV.*

Actually, you can already watch web video on your TV; it's just that the technology is a bit limited and buggy. But this is changing fast. Nearly all televisions made these days have the ability to play web video. And this technology is only going to get better.

This means your audience—your clients and prospective clients—will eventually be able to sit on their couches, flip through the web with their remotes, and pull up your videos as easily as they pull up their favorite TV shows. And if you do any type of paid-for videos, they'll be able to order those, too, on demand.

It certainly won't happen overnight, but it is expected that this convergence of web video and television will change the way we think of television.

But for you and me, the best part of all of this is that...

Web Video Levels the Playing Field for the Little Guy

Web video gives any average person the same reach, influence, and opportunities previously enjoyed only by large corporations and media companies.

For example, when in spring 2008 United Airlines broke the beloved guitar of a gentleman named Dave Carroll, he tried in vain for nearly a year to get them to make good on his damage claim. He finally became so fed up that he made a music video detailing his experience with United Airlines. It became an overnight sensation, drawing the attention of major news outlets, newspapers, and even CNN. United Airlines not only ended up with egg on their face, but got millions in free advertising—*all negative*. This would not have been possible just three years ago. Like I said, web video has leveled the playing field for the little guy.

Or let's look at television advertising, the holy grail of the advertising world. It's not cheap—well out of the reach of most small-business owners, especially for national spots. And unless you're selling a product through direct response, you have no idea how well your campaign actually performed. With web video, it's an entirely different story. You can reach a global audience at little or no cost. In fact, top video podcasters have hundreds of thousands of people view their videos *every day*. And they know much more about those viewers, from where they came from to what browser they were using.

But here's the bottom line: it's not often that a technology comes along that is accessible to everyone, doable by everyone, and desired by everyone. Web video happens to be all of those things.

People want it. They have an insatiable appetite for it. And even someone who has never touched a camera in his or her life has the ability to provide it. The only thing you have to do is pick up a camera and start. Then never quit.

After training thousands of people across the world on how to create, get traffic from, and profit from web video, I can tell you without a doubt that those who find success always follow these principles.

They stop thinking about it. They start doing it. And they never quit.

So now it's your turn. And the question you need to ask yourself is this: Would you rather look back a year from now and say, "I wish I had" or "I'm glad I did"?

"Oren Michels, CEO of Mashery, explains that 'people tend to interpret having the "right" to express themselves online as implying a lack of consequences when they say stupid things.' That's not the case."

Sharlyn Lauby,
president of Internal Talent Management

Creating a Social Media Policy for Your Organization

SO FAR WE HAVE BEEN FOCUSING on how you can person-ally have a Zen-like experience using social media. But what happens when your employees start tweeting and creating Face-book pages? What happens if they spill company secrets? What happens if they leave—and maybe not on the best of terms? The best action is to take precaution. Having a social media policy in place is akin to setting expectations. If I could sum up this whole chapter, I'd say a social media policy is about being smart and using common sense. And some companies have just that policy! So, you have two choices here. One, you can decide that you will just trust your team to use common sense and be smart about what they put online. It is simple, and lots of companies do use that method. Two, you can create and implement a more precise policy so everyone knows what the rules are. I use words like "policy" and "rules" very loosely. I think they can often con-note a very strict interpretation, but that is not what I am trying to impress here. Think of policy as "suggested guidelines" and rules as "how to play smart."

Remember, *having a social media policy in place does not mean that you get to dictate your image. But you do get to interact responsibly in the conversation that dictates your image.* And, you get to help your employees do the same. There are great benefits to today's technology and its widespread use, but there are also some risks, as dictated by Raj Malik of Network Solutions (blog.networksolutions.com/2009/sxsw-follow-up-corporate-social-media-guidelines). As Malik says, unauthorized or inappropriate commentary or posts online can:

- Get the company, and you, into legal trouble with the United States and other government agencies, other companies, customers, or the general public
- Diminish the company's brand name by creating negative publicity for the company, owners, and partners as well as yourself or your team
- Cause damage to the company by releasing nonpublic information or proprietary information
- Cost the company the ability to get patents or undermine its competitive advantage
- Cost you your job at the company

The following are 10 steps to creating your own social media policy.

1. **Decide where you stand.** A policy is only as good as the company that implements it. Essentially, the lines are drawn, and you have to take a stand. How far is your company willing to go in the social media sphere? Will you choose to communicate only in reaction to what someone else says? Will you be proactive in engaging the community (consumers and bloggers)? Without an overall attitude about social media, it can be very hard to create a policy. This doesn't have to be a verbal stance, but it should be a part of your company's culture. For example,

Zappos, a very successful online shoe store, encourages all their employees to partake in social media. In fact, 400 out of their 700 employees are on Twitter. Their stance is that everyone jumps in—and then uses his or her own common sense. It seems to be working for them so far!

2. **Determine what constitutes social media.** A blog and LinkedIn may easily be categorized as social media, but what about online video? What about Twitter? What really constitutes social media? You must have your own (preferably written) definition. This is especially true because new websites and tools emerge all the time. My personal definition of social media is any website or medium (including video) that allows for communication in the open. Let's say that you tell your employees not to mention an upcoming merger until you are ready to announce it. However, two employees chat about it with each other via direct messaging on Twitter, and because of a glitch, the message is made public. Did they break a rule or do direct messages on social media constitute a private forum?

3. **Clarify who owns what.** Does your company have a Facebook page that is handled by the head of HR? What happens when that person leaves? Who owns that page? That content? James C. Roberts III of Global Capital Group Law offers this: "If there is an offer letter or employment contract, it would normally state who owns what (usually the company). Absent that, the law could default to ownership by the company (but depending upon the state). On the other hand, if the company has turned a blind eye to personal use during work hours then it could be attacked. And, it will depend upon the extent to which what is created is based on company property (IP)." (Note: This is not to be construed as legal advice. Please consult with your own attorney for advice specific to your company.) To keep things simple, make sure your employees know what is theirs and what belongs to the company.

4. **Keep confidential information private.** Although other company policies may address the issue of keeping proprietary and personal information confidential, it never hurts to readdress it in terms of social networking. Because of the casual nature of these sites, it is easier to give away key information without realizing it. Even private messages aren't always secure. Each site has its own fallibilities. It is best to never share any confidential or proprietary information using social media—publicly or privately.

5. **Decide who is responsible.** Although it is important that everyone understands the company's social media policy, it is also important that one person or a team of people be responsible for managing social media efforts. If a customer does make a public complaint, who will answer it? Do they need to forward that to another department? Social media management doesn't automatically fall under the job description of the web developer, PR person, or HR manager. All employees should be encouraged to interact and represent the brand, but there should be one or a few who are proactively handling queries. The best way to find a social media advocate within the company is to seek out the one person or team of people who are most passionate about communicating with customers in such a manner. They may already be doing so without your knowing it. Seek out those people, and train them well.

6. **Dictate the rules of engagement without being a dictator.** It is a fine line to walk—allowing employees the freedom to engage and protecting the company at the same time. However, it can be done. You can't stop employees from communicating using the new media, but you can set some ground rules that work for everybody's benefit. Take a look at Intel's social media policy at www.intel.com/sites/sitewide/en_US/social-media.htm. The Emerging Technology Department at the Air Force has created a flowchart of

their own guidelines, which you can view at blogcouncil.
org/blog/wp-content/uploads/2008/12/air-force-blog-
assessment.jpg.

7. **Address taboo topics.** Although your employees probably
   already exercise good common sense while participating
   online, it never hurts to clarify specifically what is off lim-
   its. Raj Malik of Network Solutions offers this partial list:

   - Topics about which the company is involved in litiga-
     tion or could be in the future (e.g., policy, customer
     disputes, etc.)
   - Nonpublic information of any kind about the company,
     including, but not limited to, policies and strategy
   - Illegal or banned substances and narcotics
   - Pornography or other offensive illegal materials
   - Defamatory, libelous, offensive, or demeaning material
   - Private/personal matters of yourself or others
   - Disparaging/threatening comments about or related to
     anyone
   - Personal, sensitive, or confidential information of any
     kind

8. **Have a system for monitoring the social sphere.** A social
   media policy doesn't do much good if you don't actually
   monitor the space where the conversation is happening.
   There are plenty of free and paid tools to monitor the online space. There are also firms like ours that offer reputation management services.

9. **Make training easily available.** Think win-win. Nobody
   likes to be bossed around, especially when it comes to
   his or her own social networking. However, most people are very open to learning about how to better leverage social media sites to further their own careers and
   brands. Most people who make mistakes online just
   don't know any better. If you expect your employees to

use the social networking tools properly, you must provide training. What they put out there isn't just a reflection of the company; it is also a reflection of them. Make it a win-win for everybody.

10. **Have a crisis plan.** Let's say you have a perfect social media policy in place. What happens if an employee breaches it? What happens if the people you laid off decide to start a Facebook hate group? Or if a disgruntled customer creates a YouTube video (hey, it happened to United Airlines!)? The worst action is inaction. You must act immediately if a crisis occurs. Ignoring it—or, worse, trying to bury it—will only increase the backlash. Ideally, you have already been proactive in your efforts. You have a company blog, you have a Twitter account, and you have some influencers as friends who will vouch for your company. Either way, you will need to take corrective action right away. First, contact the person responsible. Apologize, clarify, and do what you need to do to rectify the mistake. Second, make a public announcement apologizing and clarifying. Also, address steps put into place that will keep such a debacle from occurring again. In social media, transparency is crucial. This is why step 1 is, well, step 1: decide where you stand.

> "You are in the findability department. The marketing department is dead."
>
> Todd Defren,
> *principal for SHIFT Communications*

A Final Word on Social Media

Tools for Attracting Even *More* Business

BEFORE WE FINISH UP, I want to give you a few more tools for making the most of social media marketing.

Integrating Your Social Media Efforts

One of the biggest struggles people face in marketing with social media is figuring out how it all ties together. How does social media fit in with online marketing? What does the big picture look like? You want to integrate your social media efforts not only to save time but to reach even more people than you thought possible. Let's take a look at some ways you can tie in your social media efforts.

Revolve Your Efforts Around Your Website

This is your home base—where all the action should occur. As I've mentioned, you should do everything you can to organize your social media marketing efforts around directing traffic to your website.

However, you can also use your website to let visitors know about what social media sites you're involved with, giving them the chance to keep in touch with you in other ways. Facebook, Twitter, and LinkedIn all provide badges or buttons you can place on your website, which allow visitors to connect with you on these other sites. If you have a graphic designer or are one yourself, you can create your own.

Make It Easy to Share Your Content

If you have a blog or post articles on your website, find a way to enable one-click sharing. The easier it is to share your content, the more likely it is people will share. You will reach so many more people in this manner just by leveraging your current visitors. Give your visitors an easy way for people to tell their friends. This is why I really like the functionality Word-Press provides. It is a blogging platform that you can build your entire website on. If you use WordPress, you can also download the ShareThis plug-in, which allows visitors to easily share your content on their social media sites. It can be found at www. ShareThis.com.

Social bookmarking is another way to facilitate sharing. Social bookmarking, in a nutshell, allows visitors to share their bookmarks with each other. Websites dedicated to facilitating the collection and sharing of bookmarks are a great way to attract new visitors to your website. Although there are many such sites out there, here I will focus on the three that I believe have the most potential to drive traffic to your website.

- **StumbleUpon:** StumbleUpon (www.StumbleUpon.com) is a great tool for driving long-term traffic to your website. It is my favorite social bookmarking site, because it drives quality traffic and it helps you discover quality websites. It also tends to bring a good mix of visitors.
- **Digg:** Digg (Digg.com) is a rather famous social bookmarking website, but the traffic you get from it tends to be

short-lived. Think sharp spikes of quick traffic. The audience on Digg is also partial to technology pieces.

- **Delicious:** Delicious (Delicious.com) is simple to use and has a broad audience. If you aren't familiar with social bookmarking sites and need a simple way to get started, this is a great site to get started with.

Synchronize Your Status Updates with Ping.fm or Postling.com

Status updates, across all social media sites, are crucial to presenting and sculpting your brand. However, updating all of them can be time-consuming. The best tools I have found so far for updating all your status updates at once are Ping.fm and Postling.com. Postling even provides a robust dashboard that allows you to view Facebook and Twitter comments, along with your updates, all in one place.

Initially, you have to input your login information from each of your social media sites. This takes a few minutes. Ping.fm or Postling.com then saves all the login information, and the next time you have an important message to send out, you can do so with just one click. You log in and post a single update in Ping.fm or Postling.com. Then, that update is automatically sent across the board to all the sites you gave Ping.fm or Postling.com the login information for.

There may also be search engine-related benefits to setting up Ping.fm or Postling.com that have yet to be fully unearthed. Ruth Perryman of the QB Specialists (www.TheQBSpecialists.com) sent me an email describing the way her business's Google rank shot up after she signed up for Ping.fm. I was definitely intrigued, so I interviewed Ruth.

How did you use Ping.fm to get ranked in Google for your search term?

Nobody really knows what Google uses to rank pages, and, worse, it's thought that their algorithm changes often. But my key search term "QuickBooks enterprise" shot from higher than 20 pages (I gave up looking after that) to page three within about a week of me signing up for Ping.fm and joining all the network sites they link to. I believe the links to my website from those social networking sites is the reason for the huge increase, because I didn't make any other changes during that period. We're also on the second page of Yahoo!, and on the fifth page of MSN/Live now, but I can't honestly say I knew what the ranking was before because I never checked. But I believe it's very likely they were also 20 or more pages in. We're tinkering with the website more now to see if we can replicate it. For instance, my staff is also signing up for Ping.fm. If we continue to climb up the page ranks, it'll be almost certain that this is the cause.

What is your Ping.fm strategy?

One of my friends told me about Ping.fm a few weeks back, and it sounded like a great way to manage Twitter-type messages and status updates. But I'm the anal sort (good to be when you're an accountant), so one rainy Sunday I went in and added all their networking sites that I didn't belong to. I posted my picture, added my website, and entered little bios. It never entered my mind that it might increase my ranking. But for the last six months, I've been just checking Google to see if I was in the top 20 yet, only to be denied week after week, and then, lo and behold, less than a week after I joined all those networking sites, I was suddenly on the third page. You could've knocked me over with a feather! In fact, when I saw I was also on the third page for Yahoo!, I couldn't help but yell—wait for it—"Yahoo!" Great name, by the way; very appropriate.

If you could share one tip or strategy with others looking to do the same, what would it be?

Carve out a day—a cold, rainy day over a weekend is perfect; after all, what else are you going to do?—and just start at the top of Ping.fm's list of networking sites. Join them, and complete your profiles. At the very least, put in your business name and website. It's actually a nifty little tool—you enter one 140-character post, and it'll send your post to all the microblogging and status update sites automatically (you can change your defaults so it only goes to the ones you choose). That's actually what I originally meant to use it for; the surge in page ranking was an unexpected yet delightful surprise.

Given that my company, The Marketing Zen Group, already ranks high for many of our top keywords, I have not yet tested this strategy. However, just claiming your personal name and your business name on various social media sites is a good strategy in itself. And if it does result in extra benefits, as in Ruth's case, even better!

The easiest part of social media measurement is simply counting the numbers. Website visitors, blog links, Twitter mentions, and Facebook fans are all numbers worth measuring.

Unfortunately, the numbers only tell us half of the story. Next you need to measure the sentiment of each of these social media channels. What percentage is positive versus negative? Are your efforts pushing that sentiment needle in a positive direction?

Lastly, you need to connect this all to your bottom line. You know you increased the number of mentions on Twitter, and you know that the majority of tweets were positive, but do you know how many new sales were generated as a result?

Understand this trifecta of social media measurement and you'll see success.

Andy Beal,
founder of Trackur (www.Trackur.com) and coauthor of Radically Transparent

How to Measure Your Efforts

Social media metrics is the technical term for measuring your social media marketing efforts. And, yes, this could also be a book in itself. Albert Einstein once said, "Everything that can be counted does not necessarily count; everything that counts cannot necessarily be counted." So much of social media is about building relationships and leveraging word of mouth. How do you measure goodwill? Sometimes a consumer has to hear about you 10 times before he or she will buy. You engage consumers using multiple channels, so how you do know which straw broke the camel's back?

There are some things you can measure—and you should! Here are some straightforward metrics that you can use to start measuring right away:

- **Your bottom line**: I am always surprised by how many people don't at least measure their bottom line. By "bottom line," I mean how much money you're making. How much revenue is coming in compared to how much was coming in before you started using social media?

  Social media marketing is complex, and it is sometimes almost impossible to track exactly how and why someone came to buy from you. This is because, if done correctly, social media marketing is like filling a piggy bank, each coin bringing you a bit closer to your goal. Eventually, one last coin will fill the jar; however, each coin got you a little bit closer.

  When we ask how new clients heard of us, we often get answers like, "I saw you speak once and subscribed to your newsletter. Then I befriended you on Facebook. However, I had to unsubscribe for a while, because I was busy with other things. Then I saw a status update you made on Facebook to a post you wrote, and it was exactly the help I needed." Do you get the picture? Many coins, one piggy bank. Measure your bottom line!

- **Number of leads**: This is another very straightforward

metric. How many leads did you get before you implemented social media marketing, and how many leads do you get afterward?

- **Website visits:** Currently, Twitter is responsible for 20 percent of our company's website traffic. We use Google Analytics (a free tool provided by Google) to measure how many people visited our website and where they came from.
- **Sales cycle:** Measure how long it takes to make a sale to a new client. If your best friend was selling you a car that you needed, how long would you hesitate before buying? Given that you had the money and trusted your friend, not long! Compare that to buying a car from a dealer. How many dealers would you visit? How much research would you do? Social media marketing allows you to be that friend—the person or company that people trust.

  For instance, when prospective clients come to our company, they are often already ready to buy. And these aren't small purchases. Our services start at $2,000 a month. They just have a few questions. We don't submit long drawn-out proposals or go back and forth proving that we can do the job. They already know we can, because they have seen us online. They have visited our website, read our articles, seen us on Twitter, and perhaps even seen some of my videos on Shama.TV. If you can establish your expertise online, you will find that people are more than eager to do business with you.
- **Conversion rate:** Let's say that before doing any social media marketing, one out of ten people who came to your website bought something. After you follow all the directions in this book, two out of ten people are buying. Your conversion rate just went up! Why might this be? People are more comfortable buying from brands they trust. Although you may not be Coca-Cola, you can certainly establish trust through open communication and transparency. I am more willing to buy from someone I know I can get in touch with easily than from a no-name company online. What about you?

For Executives Only! Seventeen Best Practices for Adopting Digital Marketing

Many executives between the ages of 45 and 65 are digital aliens. They were not brought up in the digital age and feel overwhelmed and sometimes fearful of the new technologies. Many struggle with the changes necessitated by engaging in digital marketing. The result is a new digital divide between companies that are fully immersed in digital applications and others that are still trying to decide if Facebook is even a good investment!

The following is a road map of 17 practices that, for the latter companies, will facilitate the adoption and successful implementation of a digital marketing program.

1. **Assess current market practices.** Determine the gaps and opportunities to position your organization in the digital world.
2. **Adopt a digital mind-set.** Gain executive understanding and buy in to the changes required to adopt a digital marketing program.
3. **Dedicate resources.** Commit staff, provide training, and allocate budget.
4. **Strategize.** Design a digital marketing strategy that incorporates your assessment, clarifies goals and brand, integrates all media, and tracks and evaluates. More than 60 percent of social media programs fail because they don't have a blueprint.
5. **Build on what you do best.** Incorporate digital media to leverage and augment successful marketing efforts already in progress.
6. **Listen, research, refine.** Monitor digital buzz and real-time customer feedback via forums, tweets, surveys, online reviews; refine your product.
7. **Give value.** Focus on giving value before expecting anything in return.
8. **Be consistent, not overpowering.** Maintain your brand; increase your digital presence through regular conversations, but don't push, overexpose, or irritate.
9. **Develop sustainable relationships.** Create conversations and take the time to interact; this is a social environment. Conversations build relationships and encourage participation. Touch your current and potential customers with regular alerts on new services, advice, and deals.
10. **Provide social sharing.** Include easy-to-access social amplification tools (social sharing buttons for Facebook, Twitter, Digg, StumbleUpon, and email) to spread the message.

11. **Cultivate satisfied, loyal customers.** Focus on caring for, thanking, satisfying, and providing value for your customers. This will engender trust and encourage your customers to do your marketing for you by sharing your product with their networks.

12. **Leverage social communities.** Access related social communities that have a potential interest in or would benefit from your product. These groups can boost exposure and penetration with little additional expense.

13. **Develop an online environment as your hub.** Drive traffic to an integrated online environment, including a website, Facebook site, landing pages, and a blog.

14. **Integrate media.** Augment your traditional advertising (TV, radio, outdoor, direct mail, print) and PR with social media, mobile, and online efforts.

15. **Monitor and measure.** Track your company's digital footprint (the size and composition of your online presence), company chatter, and social mentions.

16. **Evaluate your Social Return on Investment (SROI).** Evaluate SROI as a tool for measuring a much broader concept of value. SROI incorporates social, environmental, and economic costs and benefits into decision making and helps you readjust your strategy and tactics to meet your goals.

17. **Keep current and generate a competitive edge.** Keep your "fingers on the pulse" of your business ecosystem and the changing digital environment. This responsiveness will drive innovation and competitive positioning.

Dr. Ira Kaufman,
Entwineinc.com

Wrap-Up

To wrap up, I want to leave you with three main points to take away:

1. **Strategize first.** Before you create a single profile or partake in a single online conversation, map out your overall online strategy. What will you use to attract? What will you use to convert? What will you use to transform? The tools you use to do these things will be your tactics.

2. **Be human.** Remember that behind every Twitter name or Facebook profile is a real live human being. The ultimate goal is always to connect with that person. Even if you're talking to a group, that group comprises individuals who crave personal connection and attention.
3. **Have patience.** Measure your social media efforts, but also have patience. Social media marketing is a long-term strategy; pay attention to the results you're getting as you go, but always keep your eye on the horizon.

By now, I hope you have a much better grasp of social media marketing and what it entails. I further hope you have realized that leveraging social media isn't hard; you just have to know how to use it, and it can be an incredibly powerful tool. It is truly the Zen way of achieving success!

Burning Questions and Answers

Taking Questions and Dishing Out Answers and Advice

WHEN I WROTE THIS, I wanted to make sure I covered the topic of social media marketing in the most comprehensive and useful manner I could. To that end, I asked my blog readers to ask me their most pressing questions. Although most of their questions have already been covered in a general way in the previous chapters, I wanted to include some direct, specific answers as well. Because these questions come up often, I hope the answers will benefit you, too!

Q1: *Within the last decade, we've seen many technology trends come and go. In your opinion, why will social media marketing stand the test of time, outside of its being an exciting, dynamic, and ever-evolving way to market?*

A1: I don't know what social media will look like in another hundred years. I can say with much confidence that it will be here for many years to come. It may take on a different form, but its essence will not change. By "essence," I mean that people now know what it is like to have their own microphone—to have their opinions heard. You can't change that. You can't push and bully people anymore. People *will* talk, and today their messages can reach thousands. You want to leverage this power for the better, and that isn't going away anytime soon!

Q2: *Is social media marketing meant for all audiences? Is there a group for which it isn't a good fit?*

A2: The chances that your buyers aren't online are slim. Even if you serve geriatric patients, I can bet their caregivers still look for information on the internet. *How* they use social media can differ greatly. Do they just read articles but not interact? Or do they like having their own say? The sites they use can also vary. For this, you will have to research your audience. Two books I *highly* recommend reading on this subject are *Meatball Sundae* by Seth Godin and *Groundswell* by Charlene Li and Josh Bernoff. If you are marketing to baby boomers, *Dot Boom* by David Weigelt and Jonathan Boehman is also a fantastic read.

Q3: *Is it better to focus on traditional or social media?*

A3: It depends because the meaning of "traditional media" is changing. For example, it is quite common now for newspapers to have an online edition. Some are even focusing more on their online versions, and still others provide only online versions. I recently heard that email marketing is now considered traditional. Traditional marketing itself is evolving to encompass more and more. In the end, your focus should be on whatever medium allows you to reach your audience.

Q4: *How do I find truly qualified prospects online? I seem always to run around with circles of friends or peers. I find my colleagues more than prospects.*

A4: This is not an uncommon situation. It is easy to end up in the same circles, especially when your colleagues (and competitors) are also early adopters and use social media. The best way to expand your circle is to use Facebook groups to meet new people. You can even create your own Facebook group. If you use Twitter, you can search for people with similar interests or problems (that you can solve!). This is also why it is important to drive people to your website and collect their information there. They may not belong to your circle, but they may run into your website. Find a way to stay in touch with them.

Q5: *I get so many invites for Facebook applications! It spins my head. Do I say yes to all?*

A5: On the contrary, feel free to say no—liberally! Only say yes to applications and groups that resonate with your professional mission. Many applications force you to select at least seven friends to use the application yourself; it's one of the reasons you get so many application invites. Just say no! If you choose to just stick to the Facebook basics outlined in Chapter 4, you will be doing more than fine!

Q6: *If you have a new follower on Twitter, is it okay to invite him or her to join you on other networks? What is the proper etiquette here?*

A6: Yes, it is okay to invite people to join your other networks. *But* you shouldn't bombard them with requests or let this be your only communication with them. It's a good idea to get to know them first. Ask them what they do, and share information about yourself; build at *least* an acquaintance relationship. Otherwise, it looks like you are just trying to rack up your numbers, and no one likes being just a number.

Q7: *How do I find the time to interact with social media to really connect with people without spending all my time doing it?*

A7: First, find two social media networks to focus on. Then, come up with an online networking strategy that works for you. This doesn't have to be complex; it can consist of simple tasks. Let's look at a *simple* Facebook networking strategy: log on, update your status, wish your friends a happy birthday, respond to your messages, pick one person from your network to get to know better, and set up a call with him or her for the week. Fairly simple, right? It can be easy to lose track of time on social media sites, so you can even try setting up a timer. Once your thirty minutes are up, you are done! This does require some discipline on your part.

Q8: *What should you do if someone wants to be your friend on Facebook, but he does not tell you how he knows you or why he wants to be your friend? Is there a downside to accepting him as your friend if you don't know him?*

A8: This depends on your friending policy. I know some people who will only befriend those they know offline. Others will befriend anyone and everyone. You have to find the strategy that works for you. If you are planning to use Facebook as a way to meet new people, then you may want to consider accepting friendship requests from strangers. In my case, I reach more people through my blog and work than I meet personally. I have a wide audience, so I choose to connect with people via my fan page at www.Facebook.com/ShamaKabani. This allows me to balance privacy and accessibility. I reserve my Facebook profile only for friends I know offline.

Q9: *Does social media marketing work well for multilevel marketing businesses? I feel like my industry isn't trusted.*

A9: My experience is that social media marketing works for any type of business, but you have to figure out a way to add value to your network. Multilevel marketing schemes are an extremely misunderstood business model because of companies that ruined the industry's reputation. Social media is a great way to educate people, and you can use that to improve the way people think about multilevel marketing. Does this take time? Yes. Does it work eventually? Absolutely.

Q10: *What do you do when someone you know through your personal life posts messages on your business social media profile that don't match up with your business life?*

A10: Great question! It depends. If the message is generic or speaks to me as an individual, I don't mind it. For example, my cousins often leave "we miss you" messages on my Wall. I am okay with this. This doesn't make me less professional in other people's eyes. In fact, it humanizes me even more. On the other hand, if I receive an inappropriate message from a personal friend, I quickly delete it. If it was just a silly link, I don't say anything to her. I just delete. If I feel like she may not be up to date on Facebook etiquette, I delete her post and then message her privately, asking that in the future she contact me privately instead.

Q11: *Why do we use war terminology ("campaign," "tactics," "strategy," "target") to refer to social media as if the people we're reaching out to are our enemies, to be attacked, pillaged, and plundered?*

A11: Good point. I am not a fan of the violent connotations either. This started because traditional marketing's view of consumers was much harsher than today's view. In the earlier days, you had to *make* someone get your message. You had to convince and convert. Today, the best strategy is to present potential customers with value and choices. It's a game changer. Unfortunately, the vocabulary has stuck, because it's what we are familiar with. If I used "approach" instead of "strategy," it might confuse some readers. Not all, but some. My goal is to communicate to be understood. For now, that involves using familiar (albeit not the friendliest) vocabulary.

Q12: *How do marketers reach business owners who say that they have no time for social media? Or those that feel social media in general is a time vampire?*

A12: Give them a copy of this book. Better yet, tell them that people are social creatures (news flash) and that people are *already* talking about their businesses online. They can either be part of the conversation or not. This is a choice every business has to make. As a marketer, you can help them strategize, give them tools, and show them how to measure. The results should speak for themselves.

Q13: *How many social networking groups should someone be in?*

A13: Focus your strategy and networking efforts on a few sites at a time. Ideally, you should focus on two social networking sites and go deep. Understand the rules, cultivate relationships, and get comfortable using them for business. My experience is that most people who join smaller or niche social sites are already part of the bigger ones. It is rare to find someone joining a new social network as an early adopter who isn't already part of a bigger one like Facebook or LinkedIn.

Q14: *When supplying content to your social sites, should you repeat the same articles and blogs, or do rewrites with completely fresh material?*

A14: Share what you currently have. There is no penalty in repeating information; you don't need fresh content for each social networking site. This is a great way to propagate your information. That being said, I don't recommend repeating yourself too much. You want to share your information without seeming like an automated machine. You want to focus on sharing the same information across several media channels, not repeating the same message on one like a robot.

Q15: *How do you know which social media site gives the best ROI for your time and effort? Do I join each new one that pops up, or do I lurk, listen, and take my time?*

A15: Lurk, listen, and take your time. Don't join every network that comes your way. My recommendations are Facebook, Twitter, LinkedIn, and now Google+ as well. You can also search for specialized social networking sites that your specific audience uses.

Q16: *Any specific marketing tips for the current tough economic times?*

A16: As someone who bootstrapped my company to success, my recommendation will always be the same. Focus on marketing techniques that provide a high return on investment—like online marketing, which costs little and does a lot. Let your current clients and well-wishers be your advertising team. Encourage and reward them for sharing with their friends. Most importantly, stay optimistic. The economic tide is always changing, but people will also always have needs and wants. The only difference in a downturn is that they get extra picky. You have to educate and encourage more than you push. My employees and clients always tease me that my favorite word to use is "leverage." But it is exactly what you have to do in this economy to succeed—and what social media allows you to do with so much ease. Leverage your past success, leverage your well-wishers, and leverage your colleagues by partnering with them. Leverage social media overall to amplify your message and credibility.

> "What can't be done by advice can often be done by example."
>
> Unknown

Social Media Marketing Case Studies
Highlighting Real-World Best Practices

SOCIAL MEDIA PROFILE 1:
Yvonne DiVita, Lip-Sticking
(www.LipSticking.com)

In what ways have you utilized social media sites? If you feel blogging is the cornerstone of these efforts, do you think someone can utilize these sites without having a blog?

My foray into social media was via my blog on marketing to women. It opened the door to new and exciting relationships. I met business professionals from all over the world and even from my own backyard. I was able (and still am able) to promote myself, and my business, by sharing expertise and insight, instead of selling. After the popularity of the blog brought me speaking engagements and even client referrals, I branched out into Facebook and Twitter and some other social networking sites that I have been invited to join, such as SWOM (Society for Word of Mouth) and TwitterMoms, as well as Savvy Auntie. I find them useful in building and maintaining great relationships. And I'm able to help other women learn how to market themselves on the web. This brings me recognition as an expert in my field.

I recommend a blog. Can you make a go of it without a blog? I don't think so. A blog is the sincere, personal side of yourself and your business. The blog gives the writer an outstanding opportunity to communicate value and advice without being preachy or sales-y. On the blog, it's possible to engage numerous people in many different conversations, thereby growing your reach and connection throughout the nation and the world. With other networking sites and Twitter, you can initiate the conversation and even share select parts of it. But it all goes back to the blog, where the real opportunity to be yourself exists. Business blogging is extremely helpful for new businesses, as long as the writer remembers to focus on the business and not on too much family stuff. Be professional. If you want to have a blog for family newsletter content, start a family blog.

Which has been your favorite social media site so far and why?

I'm still a blogger at heart. I *love* Twitter. It really has extended my reach and introduced me to hundreds of new people who I can tap into if I need an answer to a simple business question or if I need content to substantiate something I am writing about in my blog. But in the end, I prefer blogs to anything else.

Do you have a social media marketing strategy?

Absolutely! If you're in business, you should never engage in social media without a strategy! Mine is to give thoughtful content and advice, and receive some in return. It's a people-policy kind of strategy—I am here to support people in their business endeavors. It's not about the tools ever! It's about the people. Anything I can do to be more personal and focused on results for others makes my work worthwhile and successful.

If you could share one tip or strategy with others looking to do the same, what would it be?

My tip would be to always remember your beginnings. In the beginning of our business ventures, we are all eager to talk to experts and take in their advice. Those experts who give freely (always maintaining a level of free advice but gently letting others know that beyond that line is paid consulting) get the best results. Be selective of those you might become a mentor to—it's a wonderful way to give back, but depending on whom you choose to mentor, the time involvement could get away from you.

I'd like to remind everyone that social media is just that: a type of connection that's social. Be sociable. Be approachable. Learn good time-management skills, and understand that no one expects the world from you. Just be the person you wished someone had been for you back when you were getting started. Do this online, via social media tools and networks, and do it offline in a true face-to-face manner. Building your business by learning how to utilize social media and how to bring it offline in a face-to-face group gathering will bring you the success you endeavor to achieve. I recently wrote a blog post that quoted Shirley Chisholm, the first African American woman elected to Congress (quoting [tennis star] Arthur Ashe): "From what we get, we can make a living. What we give, however, makes a life."

Pattie Simone, CEO of WomenCentric.net

(WomenCentric.net)

In what ways have you utilized social media marketing for your business or organization?

We use social media to share our latest blog posts, site news, and member updates, to greet/connect/interact with our members and fans. We also use social media to broaden our reach, and network by tweeting interesting/relevant articles for our members, fans/followers, and potential members/fans/followers. Topics include items of interest pertaining to women small business owners, entrepreneurs and thought leaders, social media tips, travel deals, food stories, shopping deals, etc. Basically, we broadcast, inform, interact, and promote topics, events, news, and self-produced original and outside videos relevant to our members, potential members, fans, followers, and clients.

Which has been your favorite social media site so far and why?

Twitter is our favorite social media site. We have made so many great connections and continue to meet exciting and interesting new people every day. Many of our new members have found out about us through our efforts on Twitter. The simplicity of Twitter plus the potential to reach global prospects quickly and easily really appeals to us. Twitter's reach also makes it easier to connect with a larger audience (versus what's on Facebook or LinkedIn).

Do you have a social media marketing strategy in place?

Yes: be active and engage with our Twitter, Facebook, Google+, and LinkedIn networks. Post interesting, relevant, informative pieces or discussions. Interact as close to real time as possible. Being upbeat, helpful, and engaging with our networks is definitely the most important thing—we want to be a resource for both women professionals and those searching for women professionals.

If you could share one tip or strategy with others looking to do the same, what would it be?

Use tracking analytics sites to see how your social media strategies are measuring up. We highly recommend using the bit.ly URL shortener. The data it provides is extremely valuable.

How do you measure social media ROI?

We measure our success by the strategic expansion of our core network, new member listings, media attention, and number of RTs. All our efforts support what we are doing in other channels—networking, speaking, filming, cold calling, radio, PR, etc.

SOCIAL MEDIA PROFILE 3:
Barbara Safani, Career Solvers
(CareerSolvers.com)

In what ways have you utilized social media sites?

I used Facebook to reach out to my high school classmates. The idea caught on, and other members of the school started reaching out to classmates as well. The group currently boasts several hundred members. One former classmate reached out to me to create her bio for a new website she was launching, and another contacted me to write her résumé. Both projects resulted in endorsements on LinkedIn and MerchantCircle and additional referrals. I have used Twitter to connect with the media, and as a result, I have been quoted in a syndicated column. I am also using Twitter to drive readers to my blog and my website. On LinkedIn, I have used the Answers feature to position myself as an expert and to ask recruiters specific questions that job seekers want to know the answers to. I used their responses as the basis for several blog posts. I also use LinkedIn for clients who ask for references. This has speeded up the sales process significantly.

Which has been your favorite social media site so far and why?

Facebook. It feels like you are sitting around the living room chatting it up with your friends, colleagues, and clients. It feels like the most natural medium to me and the platform that is the most fun.

Do you have a social media marketing strategy?

I use LinkedIn to establish industry relevance, promote my brand, and position myself as an expert in my field. I use Facebook to share career information and post events. I use Twitter to share important tips and links to articles and posts with my audience. I also use it to follow my competitors and thought leaders in the careers and social media space.

If you could share one tip or strategy with others looking to do the same, what would it be?

Understand that being on a social media platform requires a certain amount of transparency, and that's not a bad thing. Sometimes it makes sense to bridge the divide between your personal and professional life. When people can see another side of you, you become more real, more trustworthy, and more credible. Letting people in to your personal life (within reason) can help build your brand and help you close more sales or foster more meaningful relationships. Social media is not just a fad. Everyone should take ownership of his or her online identity, because eventually someone is going to Google you. Put your best foot forward, and manage your online presence by creating tasteful and branded profiles on the key social media sites.

SOCIAL MEDIA PROFILE 4:
Craig Drollett, Bin Ends
(www.BinEndsWine.com)

In what ways have you utilized social media sites?

We're constantly changing and upgrading what we focus on for social tools. We use Twitter for our monthly online tastings and have developed our own site, www.TwitterTaste-Live.com, as direct access to our program. We are active on Facebook as well and have recently begun video postings using the alpha of 12seconds.tv; we're currently exploring additional enhancements to both sites (www.binendswine.com and www.twittertastelive.com) that will create a much more interactive experience for our users.

Which has been your favorite social media site so far and why?

We have built the foundation of our networks on Twitter because we find that we are able to reach out to more people than with any other platform. With a quick 140-character post, we are able to reach thousands of people, literally, all over the world. Twitter and www.TwitterTasteLive.com (our online wine tasting/social media monthly series) are always the top two referrers to www.BinEndsWine.com.

Do you have a social media marketing strategy?

The issue a lot of people have with web 2.0 is not with basic use and integration but with fully understanding how to use it to disseminate a specific message. You have to adopt the lifestyle, understand why the people following you are actually following you, and understand what exactly they're hoping to get from their interaction with you. If you're constantly selling or broadcasting but not listening or interacting intelligently, then you will get tuned out. Setting up the social networks and integrating them into your own network is not a hard thing to do. The vast majority of what we use is open source and simple to integrate and upgrade. We built Twitter Taste Live based off of the Ning.com social platform. However, the ongoing project took our web design team at Saltline Studio only two days to launch.

If you could share one tip or strategy with others looking to do the same, what would it be?

Be patient, and be willing to adapt to what your users want. Don't sell, sell, sell; just get your message out, and over time you will be found.

SOCIAL MEDIA PROFILE 5:
Shel Horowitz, Principled Profit
(www.PrincipledProfit.com)

In what ways have you utilized social media sites?

To do the following:

- Build my reputation
- Build my network and develop friendships with people
- Turn some of those friendships into new income streams, speaking opportunities, etc.
- Share resources I've found (so much easier to post a tweet than go through the Digg or StumbleUpon process)
- Explore resources others have found
- Find opportunities to get covered in the media, to speak, and to pitch for work
- Vastly increase the reach of my blog by feeding it into Facebook and Plaxo
- Meet others working at the intersections between social change and marketing

Which has been your favorite social media site so far and why?

Twitter! I'm a recent convert, and I'm just amazed how easy it is to connect with people, how much useful information is exchanged, how fast my network is growing, and how helpful people are. But I find as my network grows, I miss far more than I see. I typically check three or four times a day and look two or three screens back. But now, a screen fills up in three to five minutes.

Do you have a social media marketing strategy?

More overall guiding principles: to be helpful; to put up strong content; to avoid catfights; to keep a good balance of personal, business, political, and self-promotional and to not waste my time following people who get way off on this balance; to keep trivia to a minimum; and to include some reference for context when necessary.

If you could share one tip or strategy with others looking to do the same, what would it be?

Be authentic and helpful!

SOCIAL MEDIA PROFILE 6:
Tina Su, Think Simple Now
(ThinkSimpleNow.com)

In what ways have you utilized social media sites?

I've used social media sites to expose my web content to new and existing readers. Some tips I've found useful when utilizing these sites:

- **Make many mutual friends.** Especially ones who share similar interests to those expressed on your site. Get their email addresses, and communicate with them outside of social media sites.
- **Contribute something useful to the community.** And not just spamming the site with links from your domain. Share resources and content that you've found interesting, inspiring, or useful.
- **Be personable and actively participate.** Answer emails, questions, and requests.
- **Help others.** One of my favorite sayings is, "To get what you want, help others get what they want first." It's true. Genuinely and actively help other bloggers promote their stuff; when you have something great published, they'll likely want to help you, too.

I've had great results so far. I've spent zero dollars on advertising and solely promote my site, ThinkSimpleNow.com, through social media channels. Within the first three months, the site exceeded 2,000 subscribers. Within a year, the site grew to 10,000 subscribers and 300,000 monthly page views. I am also able to earn a full-time income through the website.

Which has been your favorite social media site so far and why?
In the following order:

1. **StumbleUpon:** You can quickly gain traffic from just a few people sharing a link for your site. I also love the community on SU; people are passionate about their favorite categories. You can also consistently find useful and original content.
2. **Digg:** On the rare occasion that one of my articles hits the front page, the surge in traffic is phenomenal. It's not the traffic that I seek but the exposure that leads to new potential readers that makes Digg special.
3. **Facebook:** It gives you the opportunity to connect with people on a more personal level and follow what they're up to.
4. **Twitter:** You can easily spread useful links to many people. It's a casual and low-friction way to connect with people—even internet "celebrities."

Do you have a social media marketing strategy?

Meet and connect with as many bloggers and social media enthusiasts as possible.

If you could share one tip or strategy with others looking to do the same, what would it be?

Produce interesting, value-packed, and easy-to-understand content or services. Make it worth someone's time and attention. All these social media strategies can get you some traffic temporarily, but if you don't have the content or product to capture their attention, it's a waste of your efforts.

SOCIAL MEDIA PROFILE 7:
Adam Sell, Nine Technology

In what ways have you utilized social media marketing for your business or organization?

Since our inception about 18 months ago, Nine Technology has led a social-only strategy for lead generation. As a startup, we felt that we needed to generate buzz with these channels and try to build our partner base before spending massive amounts of cash on traditional marketing and outreach programs. We've found a great deal of success in connecting with prospects, leads, and partners on Twitter and LinkedIn, and we've amassed nearly 200 partners through this word-of-mouth and virtual word-of-mouth system.

Which has been your favorite social media site so far and why?

I personally like Twitter most of all, because it lets you get a quick thought out into the conversation. I'm a writer, and sometimes the 140-character limit can be frustrating, but it forces me to summarize my thoughts into a short sentence and invite the conversation to continue that way. My boss, however, prefers LinkedIn, because of its workplace-based focus.

Do you have a social media marketing strategy in place?

Everybody in the company has a Twitter account, and we've encouraged all employees to tweet actively from them. It took a couple of come-to-Jesus meetings to convince some of the stalwarts in the company, but we've been successful at coordinating a concerted outreach when major news is announced. I try to maintain a three-blogs-a-week policy, as that gives us plenty of content to push out the door and bring people in with.

If you could share one tip or strategy with others looking to do the same, what would it be?

Social media is neither proactive nor reactive—it's both, depending on the circumstances. Everybody will tell you "content is king," and to some degree, they're right. Without constantly churning out new things to talk about, you'll find the conversation quickly evaporating. But listening to what people say about you is of much greater consequence. Good news takes a week to travel the world. Bad news takes an hour. You need to be listening to who's saying you're doing your job right, and you need to be listening to who's saying you're doing your job wrong. They may both have valid points, and it's up to you to figure out why one's happy and the other isn't.

How do you measure social media ROI?

On a practical level, we were Hubspot clients for a long period of time, and their tools enabled us to see actual numbers on how we were doing with SEO and social media efforts. On a more observational level, though, I've found that looking at where your leads come from is indicative of how you're doing. Over time, you can watch (through Google Analytics or other such tools) where your prospects come from and where your geographic reach grows. Before this month, we hadn't had any leads from, for example, Sweden. Geographic growth is a great indicator of your message escaping beyond the website.

Chris Geier, K2
(www.K2.com)

In what ways have you utilized social media sites?

We started our entry into social media with a basic "forums and blogs" site. We had to start somewhere, and this seemed a logical step. The goal was to simply give people a place to go and ask questions, and hopefully get answers. Our hope was that we could take this simple act of socializing a problem and grow it into a vibrant interactive community utilizing a broader effort through various forms.

Once we filled a solid need with the community site, we wanted to plan out our next step. Our next effort was to establish a presence in what we saw were the three pillars of social media. Based on additional research, we also found this to be where a fair number of our "community" spent time as well.

1. LinkedIn
2. Facebook
3. Twitter

LinkedIn has a good network of people as well as active groups and discussions. We utilize LinkedIn as a way to engage in the conversation occurring about our field of expertise (Workflow and BPM). We also maintain a corporate profile to better allow people to find us and get basic information on who we are no matter where they look (e.g., Facebook, LinkedIn, Twitter, Google, etc.).

Facebook we are still experimenting with, working to figure out what works best. We initially saw a good deal of interaction and traffic on Facebook when we started engaging there. We have pages and groups created for two of our three products and use them to post basic information and news. We also use them to share event information and let people know what we are up to and how to get involved with us in some way.

Twitter has been the most versatile tool for us. We have used it extensively. Several of us have joined up and regularly interact with the community. I personally also am constantly searching out people who have questions about K2 and/or questions about related topics such as SharePoint, Workflow, BPM, and so on. If I see people asking questions about one of our products or struggling, I try to help, and I also let them know we are here if they have feedback and/or any issues. The main goal here is just to give people another avenue to interact with us. It is very important to us that we ensure if someone has a question or has feedback that he or she has a channel to voice that, regardless of time, place, format, or medium.

Which has been your favorite social media site so far and why?

My favorite social media site thus far has been Twitter. I have found it to be the most versatile and interactive. I am regularly able to interact with K2 customers and partners. We have also been very successful in expanding our community in other ways. We are regularly able to not only get feedback from our community, but also keep them informed and help link/network them together. This helps to grow our community and make it more interactive.

Do you have a social media marketing strategy?

We have a few guiding principles in social media.

1. **Open as many channels to our community as possible.** This will enable as many people in our community to interact with us in a way that is most comfortable and easy for them.

2. **Be part of the conversation.** We need to get out there and join into the discussions that are going on about not only our product but also our industry and related genres. Doing so not only helps make people aware of us, but also allows us to expand our community and help raise the interaction levels.

3. **Make all conversations open and bidirectional.** Truly look for the interaction and not just take opportunities to broadcast.

4. **Be authentic.** Do not try to hide negative information, but rather let people see it, and then let them see how you fix it.

5. **Manage the intent.** Our intent in social media is to interact and be there for people. Ensure that all decisions made map to that.

If you could share one tip or strategy with others looking to do the same, what would it be?

The primary component of any social media effort surrounds intent and authenticity. To be truly successful, a company must take a step back and understand why they are engaging in a social media effort and then must authentically follow that intent. Not being true in this effort will eventually be seen as fraudulent and greatly damage your reputation and hinder your ability to openly interact with those you seek out. I believe that to be most effective in this genre, you must be in it for the right reasons. You must be in it for the customer and to help him or her in some way. The relationship that exists between a person or entity and others in the social network must be bidirectional; both parties must benefit for it to be effective. I see too many companies out there looking to broadcast and just push information out rather than looking to truly interact and listen. They often say they are there to listen, but their true intent is often unveiled at some point.

I highly recommend before anyone ventures out there and starts talking to people through social media that he or she listen first. Get a better understanding for who people are, where they are, and what they are saying. Then seek to be part of the conversation.

Heather Whaling, Costa DeVault

(CostaDeVault.com)

In what ways have you utilized social media sites?

In December 2008, Costa DeVault partnered with the Coalition for the Homeless of Central Florida to add social media to its already strong public relations and marketing efforts. Costa DeVault assisted with initial research, listening, and strategy development. The Coalition focused on five primary goals:

1. Increase online brand recognition.
2. Reach a new demographic.
3. Increase communication, and create a dialogue with donors, volunteers, advocates, and stakeholders.
4. Position the Coalition as an authority on homelessness.
5. Encourage active involvement with the Coalition.

Per the recommendations in the plan, the Coalition created a blog, as well as Facebook and Twitter accounts. (They also established YouTube and Flickr accounts, which are in use but are not as active.) Next, the organization identified a staff person who would be responsible for monitoring and participating in social networks—in addition to her existing PR and marketing responsibilities. Specifically, her mission was to participate in social networks to connect with local residents and businesses.

Which has been your favorite social media site so far and why?

The combination of Facebook, Twitter, and the blog have worked well for the Coalition. One by itself wouldn't be nearly as effective. The Coalition has been able to leverage the interplay between the three networks and the Coalition's existing website, each of which reaches a different audience, providing opportunities to repurpose content. Instead of reinventing the wheel, a blog post can be shared on Twitter and Facebook. Likewise, a Flickr album can be posted to all three networks. By understanding how the sites complement each other, the Coalition has been able to extend their social media efforts to three networks without generating three times the work.

Do you have a social media marketing strategy?

Yes! Costa DeVault and the Coalition are firm believers in taking a strategic approach to social media. After all, you need to be able to justify that time spent on Twitter or blogging is a good use of resources. For the Coalition, that meant establishing measurable objectives, such as "increase web traffic by 10 percent," "be mentioned on outside blog posts at least 12 times per year," and "obtain bulk donations of specific in-kind items at least three times a year from social media 'asks.'"

To ensure their efforts aligned with their objectives, the Coalition began the process with research. Before participating in any online conversations, the Coalition took the time to understand which networks are most used by the people they're trying to reach. In addition, the Coalition listened to conversations already taking place to familiarize themselves with each network's subculture—a key part to social media success.

After the research phase, the Coalition laid the groundwork for their own social media efforts, created employee guidelines for social media participation, created profiles on targeted sites, and began to add content and participate in discussions. Evaluation is a key component to their social media engagement. Is their network growing? Are people engaging and interacting with the content they create? Is traffic to their website increasing? Is the network strong enough to make in-kind donations?

If you could share one tip or strategy with others looking to do the same, what would it be?

Many nonprofits and businesses don't have the resources to create an entire "social media department." Instead, they need to integrate social media into their current responsibilities. A tip to make that more manageable: instead of creating a profile on every network, begin by engaging just a few. Get the hang of those, become a valued member of the network, and then think about expanding your presence. The Coalition chose Facebook, Twitter, and blogging because they align with their overall goals. Yes, you need to monitor keywords on other networks, but that doesn't mean you need to maintain an active presence everywhere. For most organizations, that's just not realistic.

The Coalition can provide a litany of statistics to illustrate the value of their social media efforts—including Twitter followers; Facebook fans; blog traffic, which continues to increase every month; and inbound links. But the most effective way to demonstrate the value of social media isn't in these metrics. Social media matters to the Coalition because when they needed extra help, their online network—people who were strangers just months ago—stepped up to the plate.

The economic turbulence led to a drastic drop in food donations from individuals and in the food supplies available from local food banks. To help meet the shortage facing the Coalition, they decided to test the strength of their online network by launching a bold challenge to the local community: the "Orlando 'Can' Care Challenge." This social-media-driven food drive was promoted via Twitter, Facebook, and the organization's blog.

During the weeklong challenge, the Coalition tweeted and Facebooked updates as new donations were brought in and posted photos to Flickr of each donation or group. By the end of the week, with only a few hours of staff time invested in the project, the Coalition was surprised to learn that their network produced 1,000 pounds of food.

That's just one example that illustrates why the time spent building and cultivating an online network is time well spent for the Coalition for the Homeless.

SOCIAL MEDIA PROFILE 10:
Father Chris Terhes,
Romanian Greek-Catholic Association
(RoGca.org)

In what ways have you utilized social media sites?

We used the social media websites to find and get in touch with the proper people who could become sympathetic to our cause and help us bringing awareness about the discrimination and persecution of the Greek-Catholic minority in Romania.

Our activity is a little bit different from that of most of the nonprofit organizations in the United States; therefore I would like to briefly describe what we do so that you can better understand why and how we used the social media websites.

The Romanian Greek-Catholic Association, of which I am president, supports the Greek-Catholic minority in Romania, which is currently facing a cultural and religious cleansing. In 1948 the communist regime abolished the Greek-Catholic Church in Romania and persecuted its bishops, priests, and believers for their religious views. After the fall of communism in Romania in 1989, despite the fact that our Church was recognized again by the government, the discrimination and persecution continued, hundreds of thousands of Greek-Catholic believers continuing to have their rights violated. Along with the pressure on our people, the Romanian government started a national campaign to destroy the Greek-Catholic heritage, tens of our churches being demolished or destroyed in the last two decades. The U.S. Department of State reported these violations and abuses against our community in many reports during the years.

The main challenge that we had was the fact that most Americans didn't know anything about these abuses taking place in Romania; therefore, the first thing that we did was to build a website to expose this situation. The website was optimized for search engines, and we used many of the techniques related to search engine marketing in order to get more exposure to our website and have it well ranked for certain keywords that were related to our cause.

Our first approach after the launch of the website was to use the regular media to expose the situation in Romania. We sent a press release out using one of the media wire websites. We also sent the press release directly to the main newspapers in the United States, but the exposure was very limited.

Considering the amount that we paid to distribute the press release versus the return in coverage, we soon realized that this is not the path to go if we want to help our community in Romania. We learned from experience (and out of our own pocket) that in the long term, it is better to build a relationship with somebody who writes about a subject related to our cause and make that person aware this way about the situation in Romania than to just spam him or her with press releases. This is the moment when we switched the strategy and we started using the social media websites to find and get in touch with people who could become supportive of our cause.

We started using LinkedIn, Facebook, and Twitter to find journalists, bloggers, or any other type of writers who were writing about religious affairs, foreign affairs, human rights, or any other domain that was connected somehow to our cause.

Using this approach, we were able to find and get in touch with a lot of writers; many of them asked for more details about the situation in Romania, and some of them even wrote a piece or republished our press releases. This was a great chance for me to establish a personal relationship with many of them. We had many of them assisting us with advice or even helping us writing press releases. One of them recently started her own radio talk show and invited me for an interview by the end of September. Without the social media websites, I don't think we would've been able to find so many people supportive of our cause.

Which has been your favorite social media site so far and why?

In our case, the social media website that helped us the most was LinkedIn.

We were using Facebook and Twitter as well, but LinkedIn was by far the best website to find and get in touch with people who could help our cause.

We had a very specific group of people that we initially targeted, and LinkedIn offered us the best solution to find them.

I was amazed by the search options provided by LinkedIn as well as by the search results. Because there are so many search options, you can target your search very well. Also, the groups on LinkedIn offer you a very good chance to know experts and to follow discussions from certain fields. The Q&A option on LinkedIn offers you the chance to get advice from some of the best experts out there. I myself posted few questions on LinkedIn, and I was amazed by how many people offered their expertise on the issue that I addressed.

If you really want to get in touch with professionals and learn from them, I would strongly recommend LinkedIn.

Do you have a social media marketing strategy?

I would rather say that I have certain rules that I follow instead of a defined social media marketing strategy. Because of the rapid changes in the technology, web applications, and new tactics that are discovered for how to use these new web applications, it is very hard to write a strategy in stone. Here are a few of the rules that I follow:

- **Objective.** Before you start planning anything, you have to decide exactly what your goal or objective that you want to achieve is.

- **Know the appropriate tactics that you can use or afford to achieve your objective.** If you have enough money, you can hire a PR firm to take care of everything for you. If you don't, then you have to identify from the tactics available out there those that you can use or afford to accomplish your objective. For example, you can send a press release to all the journalists in the United States using one of the newswire services available online, but it will cost you a few thousand dollars. This tactic might be very effective for your cause, but can you afford it?
- **Planning.** Once you've defined the clear objective and identified the tactics that you can use, you have to create a plan or a strategy for how to use these tactics to achieve your goal.
- **Execution.** Put your plan in action.
- **Stay informed.** Try to stay up to date with news related to social media marketing. New tactics can be developed in this field that you were not aware of when you started your campaign.
- **Be flexible.** Learn from your own mistakes, and adjust your plan. This might include adjusting the tactics that you use, either because you realized that one of them is not working or because a new one was developed, or changing your objective because you realized that it is unachievable.

If you could share one tip or strategy with others looking to do the same, what would it be?

Before you start your campaign, find out the story behind the campaigns that were successful as well as those that failed. It is better to learn from somebody else's mistake than from yours.

Social networking means interacting with people virtually. But like when you interact with people face-to-face, the other person can react in a different way from what you expected. Keep your good manners, and don't take it personally; just move forward.

Karen Maunu, Love Without Boundaries

(www.LoveWithoutBoundaries.com)

In what ways have you utilized social media sites?

We started by using a blog to tell the stories of the kids. Telling the stories of the children is so important, because it shows the true difference that is being made. In December 2008, our website was hacked into, and for a while we were without a website. We were still receiving children who needed care—some who needed emergency surgery—for whom we could no longer raise funds. Someone told us about the Facebook Giving Challenge sponsored by the Case Foundation that was through Facebook Causes. We are all moms, and none of us had a Facebook page at that time, but our kids did. We braved this brand new world of social media to see if there would be any way we could compete in this contest. It didn't take long before we were helping to sign up all of our friends, family, and anyone else who would help. To win the contest, you had to make at least a $10 donation for your vote to be counted. There was a daily contest of the most unique donations, and each day you could win $1,000 (we won 13 times), and then over the whole contest period (50 days), the most unique voters would win $50,000—and we won! We had so many people helping—college students going up and down dorm floors, nurses who brought their computers to work, people who sat in Starbucks trying to get voters. We had a slogan: for $10 you can save 10 lives. In China, a heart surgery is $5,000, so winning $50,000 meant we could heal 10 children—and we did.

This was the start of our social media success. We are now using our Cause page to update people on the children we are helping, and we get donations almost on a daily basis. We also have over 14,000 people following us. We feel that because we were already an online virtual foundation, it really helped us to mobilize people to be able to help with getting people to help.

We post stories of the kids on our Facebook Cause page and also on our own FB pages. Our stories become viral in that once a story or a photo is posted, many other volunteers or supporters will post it on their pages, too. Social media has become larger than just one person posting; it has become a community of people spreading our stories.

The success on Facebook has helped us to launch into other sites, too. We are also using Twitter and LinkedIn. Twitter has also been very successful for us, allowing us to personally connect with people and tell our story.

Which has been your favorite social media site so far and why?

Facebook, because we are able to actively get donations from our supporters and share the stories of our kids. From this, our stories are spread all over—so many more people are learning about what LWB does by each of us posting in addition to our Cause page. It is a great place for people to stay updated on what we are doing.

Do you have a social media marketing strategy?

Love Without Boundaries has been well known in the Chinese adoption community, and our goal for social media has been to break outside of this group and to have more people know about our work. When we started branching outside the adoption world, our goal was try to get as many people as possible to learn about our work. We wanted people to see how hard we work and to learn about how this virtual worldwide foundation of over 150 volunteers from 12 countries and 36 states is able to help more than 1,500 children a year. We knew that if people could just hear about us, they would want to learn more and help. It is working! We also want to educate people on adoption and let people know how to adopt. So far, at least one family I talked to on Twitter is in the process of adopting.

Love Without Boundaries is an almost all-volunteer foundation. To keep our overhead the very lowest possible, we don't have an office. We all work out of our homes. Social media has become an extension of how we were already working—online. The Facebook staff and the Case Foundation were shocked that a small charity of moms was able to win against the "big" charities. The reason that we were able to was because we already did so much work online.

If you could share one tip or strategy with others looking to do the same, what would it be?

The one tip that we would offer is to be genuine, honest, and transparent. When people can see who you really are, they will join in and start to spread your message, too. It is like a large bandwagon that others start hopping on, and with this, your message starts spreading far and wide.

SOCIAL MEDIA PROFILE 12:

Justin Winter, Cofounder of DiamondCandles.com

(DiamondCandles.com)

In what ways have you utilized social media marketing for your business or organization?

We utilized social media (Facebook most readily) to test our innovative product idea back in February of this past year, receive feedback about our products, develop our refined product after our minimum viable product launch, create a community that encourages fans and customers to come back very regularly, and develop ongoing feedback about future scents to aid us in our new product development.

Do you have a social media marketing strategy in place?

We make earth-friendly, all-natural soy candles that each contain a ring worth either $10, $100, $1,000, or $5,000. Because people have the excitement of not knowing which type of ring is inside their candle, an extremely high percentage of our thousands of customers take pictures of their rings once they get them out of their candles and upload those pictures to our Facebook page. This encourages people to come back and see the latest posted rings and who received rings worth $100+. We commonly hear that people are becoming "addicted" to Diamond Candles and our Facebook page, coming back to our page multiple times a week to see the latest "ring reveal" pictures. We have also encouraged and successfully utilized video with YouTube where people record "ring reveal" videos of them pulling their rings out of their candles and showing them to the camera.

Which has been your favorite social media site so far and why?

We would say that Facebook has certainly been our "home base" in terms of engagement and reaching our existing fans and those friends in their networks. We have a social media marketing strategy in place that has been extremely sucsessful to the point of close to 100 user-generated videos on YouTube and over 37,000 fans on Facebook.

If you could share one tip or strategy with others looking to do the same, what would it be?

Create value in your product or service that inspires people in some way and then figure out a way to utilize social media to bring together people who have a passion for your products and services. Simply having a good social media strategy with the latest tools will do nothing if you have bland undistinguished products that no one cares about. Good products can't help but be successful even with a nominal social media strategy.

How do you measure social media ROI?

For ROI we frequently use Facebook to drive traffic to different pages on our site, so that we can measure traffic via Google Analytics as well as measure that traffic against sales: for example, every visitor we get directly from YouTube is worth approximately X dollars.

Discussion Questions

A Guide to Sparking Engagement on the Topic of Social Media

WHEN I WROTE the first edition of this book, I never could have guessed that in addition to being a guide for business leaders, it would also come to serve as a popular textbook on the topic of social media. Emails, tweets, and messages from professors and students around the world inspired me to add this chapter. Whether you are trying to assess your own social media strategy or using this text to teach others, I hope you will find this addition helpful.

1. Why is determining your target audience so crucial?
2. How can a website attract, convert, and transform at the same time?
3. What does it mean to use the right online "voice" for your brand?
4. How can you make a blog compelling for your audience?

5. What does the search engine optimization (SEO) process entail?
6. How do you perform keyword research?
7. What is the difference between a Facebook profile, page, and group? When is each best utilized?
8. In the age of social networks, why does a website still matter?
9. What should an ideal social media policy address?
10. Why is the audience's brand more important than the company's brand online?
11. How can an organization build around the identity of their target market?
12. How can you best engage an audience on Facebook?
13. What is your personal philosophy or friending policy on social media?
14. What are the elements of a strong LinkedIn profile?
15. How does Twitter differ from LinkedIn and Facebook?
16. What are some best practices when utilizing hashtags on Twitter?
17. How are social and search merging? (Think: +1 on Google Plus)
18. What is a personalized search?
19. What are the elements of a strong online video?
20. What are a few things a company's internal social media policy should address?
21. What are some ways in which a company can monitor and boost their online reputation?
22. Why is listening so important on the web?
23. What are some metrics through which social media return on investment (ROI) can be measured?
24. What is the best way to handle a negative review or comment on a social network?
25. How do you think social media will evolve in the next two years? Five years?

Index

About the Author

Web and TV show host. Bestselling author. International speaker. Award-winning CEO of The Marketing Zen Group—a global online marketing firm. Shama is the face of today's digital world, and represents the best her generation has to offer. She has aptly been dubbed the "master millennial of the universe" and "an online marketing shaman" by Fast Company.com.

Shama holds a master's degree in Organizational Communication from the University of Texas at Austin, and prides herself in being a constant learner. Through her web marketing company, Shama works with businesses and organizations around the world. In 2009, BusinessWeek honored Shama as one of the Top 25 under 25 entrepreneurs in North America. In 2010, Shama won the prestigious Technology Titan Emerging Company CEO award. In 2011, *Entrepreneur* magazine featured her as one of four Super Sonic Youth, dubbing her a "Zen Master of Marketing." In 2012, Shama's company, The Marketing Zen Group, was honored at the White House for being named to the Empact100 List of the top U.S. companies run by a young entrepreneur.

When not working directly with her clients or shooting shows for the media, Shama travels the world speaking on business, entrepreneurship, and technology.

Shama resides in Dallas with her family, which includes her husband, Arshil, her dog, Snoopy, and her cat, Maui. *The Zen of Social Media Marketing* is Shama's first book. This is the third edition.

You can reach Shama:

> By email: Shama@MarketingZen.com
> On Facebook: www.Facebook.com/ShamaKabani
> On Twitter: www.Twitter.com/Shama
> On LinkedIn: www.LinkedIn.com/in/ShamaHyder
> On Google+: GPlus.to/shama